CORE SKILLS

Information Technology

WRTC L̶ ̶ ̶ ̶ ̶ ̶

FUR

Enterprise

GNVQs

Business
Management Studies
Retail & Distributive Services
Information Technology

PETER ROBINSON

CONTENTS

INTRODUCTION

The importance of information technology

Information is and always has been valuable. Without good information it is difficult to make intelligent decisions. Information technology (the handling of information by electronic means) is transforming our jobs and lives. In the UK, more than 7 million people use information technology substantially at work. This increase in the use and accessibility of information technology is transforming work roles and patterns and creating demands for new skills.

In the past, large businesses had Data Processing or Computing Departments with expensive mainframe computers and employed highly specialised and skilled staff to operate them. Now, many of these mainframe computers are being replaced by micro-computers on office desks (computing power is one of the few commodities that is falling in cost each year).

The use of information technology has allowed an incredible explosion in the amount of data available. For example, it is estimated that today's 9,000 daily newspapers contain some 300,000 characters each; totalling 2.7 billion characters per day. Such a deluge of data creates problems for those who design and use information systems. For instance, the space agency NASA is said to have analysed only 3 per cent of the data it has collected – the deterioration of the ozone layer could have been detected earlier from data that was routinely gathered but insufficiently analysed.

People's ideas about computers and the use of information technology have changed a great deal too. However, as is often the case with technological innovation, misconceptions do remain – it was once thought that to travel faster than 30 mph would kill train passengers!

Information technology skills in context

To help you understand and prepare for the use of information technology in real life, the skills in this book are placed in a practical context. The context is an organisation called *Freedom Holidays*, where there is a real need to use IT (information technology). *Freedom Holidays* is closely based upon a real organisation, although the name and a few details have been changed. The nature of their work is particularly relevant to all those doing GNVQ qualifications in:

- Health & Social Care
- Hospitality & Catering
- Leisure & Tourism

All learners studying for GNVQ qualifications must demonstrate their competence in IT. This book is intended to develop their information technology skills and those of students in related vocational areas – you do not *have* to be a GNVQ or NVQ student to learn about IT as a core skill.

What you need to know

This book presumes you have had very little experience of using computers. All you need to know is

- how to switch on a computer
- how to use the main keys on the keyboard
- how to get into a program
- how to get out of a program
- how to switch off or log off

It is also assumed that you will have access to manuals, but hopefully you will not need to use them very much. You may get help from friends or fellow students – this can be very valuable.

How to use this book

Step 1: select the *level* of Information Technology you wish to achieve (at least level 2 for Intermediate GNVQs, at least level 3 for Advanced GNVQs – if you are uncertain, consult a *tutor*) and study the *Information Technology Specifications* (see pages 6–13) to understand clearly which skills you need to practise and improve.

Step 2: turn to the *Practice Activities* to practise these skills. If you need help, turn to the *Help Section* at the back of the book.

Step 3: when you are ready, complete *assignments* (following the suggestions made in the *Evidence Opportunities* section and/or set on your GNVQ course) to produce evidence of achievement. If you wish to be assessed, you should consult a tutor before or during the assignment work.

Step 4: once you have successfully completed an assignment, make sure you record your achievement.

If you are a novice, work through the *Practice Activities* in the order they are presented. The tasks get more complicated as you progress. The later, more complex ones assume things that have been explained in the earlier ones.

Experienced IT users

If you are already familiar with information technology, and have used it in a variety of contexts, look carefully at the *Information Technology Specifications* (pages 6–13) and identify any gaps in your skills that you need to fill. Turn to the appropriate *Practice Activities* to practise the skills you need, and then select the assignments in the *Evidence Opportunities* section that you need to complete. (It may well be that you will need to do *all* the assignments for the appropriate level.)

The Information Technology specifications explained

The specifications for Information Technology require you to handle three types of information: *text*, *numbers* and *graphics*. You need to show that you can **prepare**, **process** and **present** *all* three.

The specifications are made up of four elements:
1) Prepare information
2) Process information
3) Present information
4) Evaluate the use of information technology

Every element, no matter at what level, relates to one of these four functions, and all these functions are inter-related:

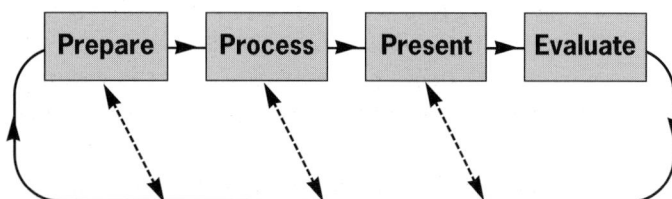

The emphasis of the specifications is upon the ability to use facilities found within broad 'families' of applications (spreadsheets, databases, word processing, desktop publishing, graphics) not upon specific software. As software programs become more powerful and versatile the boundaries between the applications become increasingly difficult to determine. Some of the more sophisticated programs incorporate facilities from two or more applications. Use computer programs that are widely available – you are not expected to write your own.

HELP
If you need help understanding terms such as spreadsheats, databases, word processing, desktop publishing and graphics, turn to *The Help Section* (pages 98–128).

Element 1: Prepare information

> **Requirements:**
> **Level 2**: Input information appropriate for a task and store input systematically.
> **Level 3**: Configure software to aid input of information as appropriate for a task.

For this element you are required to input textual, graphical and numerical information. Evidence of textual input could be collected from a variety of applications, such as word-processing and desktop publishing. To demonstrate numerical input, you could use a spreadsheet or accounting program. You could also use a database, as long as it has a facility to manipulate numbers. You could provide evidence of graphical input by creating shapes and objects using a drawing/painting program or a CAD program, or you could create lines and boxes and images within a desktop publishing or advanced word-processing program.

You are also expected to recognise errors and faults and respond accordingly.

At level 3 you will be expected to 'customise' software (e.g. set up templates and style sheets).

Element 2: Process Information

> **Requirements:**
> **Level 2**: Process and combine information appropriate to a task.
> **Level 3**: Create automated routines and combine information appropriate to a task.

This element is concerned with the manipulation and combination of information.

To demonstrate capability, you are required to edit, organise and integrate textual, graphical and numerical information. Evidence of textual manipulation should include the use of search/replace, and formatting facilities such as justification, tabulation and setting margins. Examples of graphical manipulation could include changing lines and boxes, or the size and location of images. To show manipulation of numerical information you should include use of formulas and the creation of charts and tables.

At level 2 you do need to demonstrate some integration of information. You can do this relatively easily – e.g. by importing text and images into a document, or organising a mailshot.

Level 3 includes the creation of automated routines to help in the manipulation of information. Automated routines are tools which allow repetitive sequences of operations to be programmed into single operations, such as macros, batch files, mail-merge, database query and report routines. If you are not sure what these terms mean do not, at this stage, worry. Many of them are illustrated in the *Practice Activities*.

In addition, at level 3 you are expected to access information from remote sources (i.e. information held on other computers). You can achieve this via a network or by using telecommunications.

Element 3: Present information

> **Requirements:**
> **Level 2**: Present combined information appropriate to a task.
> **Level 3**: Organise information for presenting appropriate to a task.

For this element you are required to present textual, graphical and numerical information, some of which has been combined.

To demonstrate capability you need to integrate different sources of information and ensure that the format of the combined output is coherent and consistent. For instance, the screen display and printout should be designed so that the information is clear and arranged in manageable portions; there should be no output across perforations of continuous stationery; and tables should be easy to read. Most documents should include information such as the date, page numbers and filename (these can often be generated automatically).

At level 3 you need to present information, taking into consideration factors such as the audience for which it is intended and its 'fitness for purpose'. For instance, information designed for a notice board in a reception area will differ in content and appearance to that intended for a staff-room notice board.

Element 4: Evaluate the use of information technology

> **Requirements:**
> **Level 2**: Examine own and others' uses of information technology.
> **Level 3**: Evaluate alternative ways of using information technology.

This element requires you to look at the original intentions and expected outcomes of the use of information technology to see what has been achieved, and to consider what worked and what didn't. Evaluation should be ongoing throughout all activities concerned with preparing, processing and presenting information. It should include a comparison of the speed, ease of use, effort and accuracy of using information technology with the speed, ease of use, effort and accuracy of using manual methods.

As well as specific comparisons, this element requires you to have a more general overview of information technology.

For instance, at level 2 you are expected to evaluate the the relevance of applications to everyday working. Furthermore, you are expected to be able to select optional facilities available in order to improve efficiency (e.g. the storing of search routines).

At level 3 you need to be able to compare IT usage with non-IT means of handling information. You also need to consider the overall application – as a system – not just the configuration of one piece of software.

At both levels you are required to recognise the implications of good working practices and health & safety issues (such as light, noise, heat, strain and stress) and basic errors and faults.

The 1995 specifications

On the following pages you will find the specifications for Information Technology at level 2 and at level 3. Use them as a reference while you are working through the *Practice Activities* and *Evidence Opportunities* to ensure that you are fulfilling the Performance Criteria and Range (these are explained in *Evidence Opportunities*). At the bottom of each page the practice activities and evidence opportunities are linked to the Performance Criteria to give you an idea of what you can achieve by completing them.

Software (PC2) for text, an example is word processing; for graphics, examples are drawing software and painting software; for number work, examples are spreadsheet software and accounts software. Databases could be used to cover both textual and numerical information; desktop publishing could be used to cover both textual and graphical elements.

Easy to edit (PC2) this includes, for example, the appropriate use of returns and tabs, and the use of a suitable numerical format when numbers are used for calculation.

Information developed during input (PC1 range) this is information which does not exist in hard-copy form before input, but is put together during the process of input, for example formulas, drawings, ideas or a letter to be drafted.

Graphics (PC1 range) this includes, for example, pictures, photographs, drawings and scanned images stored digitally, as well as the software tools for creating new images.

Level 2 Specification

Element 2.1: Prepare information

PERFORMANCE CRITERIA

A student must:

PC1 select information appropriate to the task

PC2 enter information into **software** in ways that will make it easy to edit

PC3 keep source information required for the task

PC4 store input systematically and make backup copies

RANGE

Select: information taken from existing sources, information developed during input

Information: text, graphics, numbers

Enter: inputting source information accurately, making immediate corrections to errors noticed on entry, putting right simple equipment faults, using manuals and on-line help facilities, asking for help as appropriate

Software: for text, for graphics, for numbers

Store input systematically: naming files sensibly to indicate the contents, locating files conveniently for subsequent use, creating and using directories to group related files, saving work before and after important changes, saving work when all the information has been input

Tasks (PC1 and PC3) these are activities which are relevant to the settings in which the student is working and where the use of information technology is judged by the student to be necessary or helpful. They will usually involve work which relates to the requirements of all of the elements in the unit and in many cases to other core skills and vocational units. Examples at this level include producing a newsletter incorporating text, pictures and a table of figures; creating a questionnaire and using a database or spreadsheet to enter and process the information collected, leading to graphs and tables to show survey results; producing a poster, publicity material and a personalised mailshot for a fund-raising event, together with a database of helpers and the kinds of help offered.

Backup copies (PC4) work saved on a separate storage medium, for example, a floppy disk.

Existing sources (PC1 range) examples include printed documents such as price lists or catalogues containing information to go into a database, or images to be scanned. Other examples may be written in longhand, such as notes of a meeting to be word-processed or readings from a survey or experiment that need to go into a spreadsheet.

Errors (PC2 range) examples include typing mistakes that can be corrected before the return key is pressed. Other examples are an attempt to input a word instead of a date, or to input a number that is too big.

Simple equipment faults (PC2 range) for example, those caused by poorly connected cables, equipment being switched off or wrongly set up.

	Practice Activity	Evidence Opportunity
PC1	2, 3, 4, 5, 6, 7, 9, 10, 13, 16	2, 3, 4, 5, 6, 7, 8, 10, 11, 12
PC2	2, 3, 4, 5, 6, 9, 13, 16	2, 3, 4, 5, 6, 7, 8, 11, 12
PC3	4, 5, 6, 13, 16	5, 7, 12
PC4	5, 13	4, 6, 10

Software (PC2 and PC3) for text, an example is word processing; for graphics, examples are drawing software and painting software; for number work, examples are spreadsheet software and accounts software. Databases could be used to cover both textual and numerical information; desktop publishing could be used to cover both textual and graphical elements. CD-ROM software could be used to provide textual, graphical and numerical information.

Make calculations (PC3) for example, use a formula in a spreadsheet or total numerical fields in a database.

Resolving differences of format (PC6) the imported material should look natural in its new location. Examples of differences include different fonts, margins, tab settings, paragraph layouts, sizes and/or shapes of graphics, forms of tables, formats of numbers.

Sorting (PC4 range) examples include sorting records in a database or rows in a spreadsheet.

Importing (PC6 range) examples include bringing information from another source into the file being processed, pulling a picture from a drawing file into a desktop-published file of text, using electronic mail to download information into a file.

Level 2 Specification

Element 2.2: Process information

PERFORMANCE CRITERIA

A student must:

PC1 **find information** required for the task

PC2 use appropriate **software** to **edit information**

PC3 process numerical **information** by using **software** to make calculations

PC4 **reorganise information** as required for the task

PC5 save work at **appropriate intervals**

PC6 **combine information** from different sources, resolving differences of format

RANGE

Find: by looking in the right directory, by looking for files with a given name, by searching for information which meets specified criteria

Information: text, graphics, numbers

Software: for text, for graphics, for numbers

Edit: amending, moving, reformatting, copying, deleting, inserting

Reorganise: sorting, restructuring stored information

Appropriate intervals: before and after important changes, when the processing is complete

Combine: importing information of the same type, importing information of a different type

Tasks (PC1 and PC4) these are activities which are relevant to the settings in which the student is working and where the use of information technology is judged by the student to be necessary or helpful. They will usually involve work which relates to the requirements of all of the elements in the unit and in many cases to other core skills and vocational units. Examples at this level include producing a newsletter incorporating text, pictures and a table of figures; creating a questionnaire and using a database or spreadsheet to enter and process the information collected, leading to graphs and tables to show survey results; producing a poster, publicity material and a personalised mailshot for a fund-raising event, together with a database of helpers and the kinds of help offered.

Specified criteria (PC1 range) the search criteria will be specified by the student to meet the requirements of the task, for example 'sex = female and age <25'.

Reformatting (PC2 range) this includes both operations on individual items, for example underlining a word or converting a number to currency format, and operations concerning larger collections of information, for example changing paragraph layout, the style of shading in a diagram, or the sizes of columns in a table.

Restructuring (PC4 range) examples include changing the sequence in which rows or columns in a spreadsheet are organised, reorganising text under headings and subheadings, reorganising information from a database as required for the task.

	Practice Activity	Evidence Opportunity
PC1	3, 5, 6, 10, 12, 14, 16	8, 9, 13
PC2	2, 3, 4, 5, 6, 9, 13, 15, 16	5, 6, 7, 8, 9, 12
PC3	6, 13, 15	5, 7, 10
PC4	5, 6, 7, 10, 12, 13, 15, 16	6, 7, 8, 10, 12, 13
PC5	2, 3, 4, 5, 6, 7, 9, 10, 13, 15, 16	2, 3, 4, 10, 11
PC6	3, 10, 16	7, 12

Tasks (PC1) these are activities which are relevant to the settings in which the student is working and where the use of information technology is judged by the student to be necessary or helpful. They will usually involve work which relates to the requirement of all of the elements in the unit and in many cases to other core skills and vocational units. Examples at this level include producing a newsletter incorporating text, pictures and a table of figures; creating a questionnaire and using a database or spreadsheet to enter and process the information collected, leading to graphs and tables to show survey results; producing a poster, publicity material and a personalised mailshot for a fund-raising event, together with a database of helpers and the kinds of help offered.

Combined information (PC4) screen display and print-out should be designed so that the information is clear and is arranged in manageable portions. There should be no output across page breaks or perforations of continuous stationery and tables should be easy to read.

Information referencing (PC1 range) many documents should include references, for example, date, page numbers and titles. These can often be generated automatically.

Level 2 Specification

Element 2.3: Present information

PERFORMANCE CRITERIA

A student must:

PC1 present **information** in different ways and select which way best meets the **requirements** of the task

PC2 use appropriate **software** to display **information**

PC3 use appropriate **software** to produce hard copy of **information**

PC4 present combined **information** in a consistent format

PC5 store **information** in files and make backup copies

RANGE

Information: text, graphics, numbers

Requirements: fitness for purpose, matched to audience, clarity, accuracy, appropriate use of information referencing, consistent format

Software: for text, for graphics, for numbers

Software (PC2 and PC3) for text, an example is word processing; for graphics, examples are drawing software and painting software; for number work, examples are spreadsheet software and accounts software. Databases could be used to cover both textual and numerical information; desktop publishing could be used to cover both textual and graphical elements.

Backup copies (PC5) work saved on a separate storage medium, for example, a floppy disk.

	Practice Activity	Evidence Opportunity
PC1	3, 7, 10, 13, 15, 16	4, 7, 8, 10, 12
PC2	2, 3, 4, 5, 6, 7, 9, 10, 13, 15, 16	2, 4, 5, 9, 12
PC3	2, 3, 4, 5, 6, 7, 9, 10, 13, 15, 16	2, 4, 5, 6, 7, 8, 10, 11, 12
PC4	3, 10, 16	8, 14
PC5	5, 10, 12, 13, 16	4, 6, 12, 13

Reasons (PC1) examples include making things more effective or easier when processing a large volume of information when undertaking an activity which will take a long time to perform manually, or when storing large amounts of information.

Tasks (PC3) these are activities which are relevant to the settings in which the student is working and where the use of information technology is judged by the student to be necessary or helpful. They will usually involve work which relates to the requirements of all of the elements in the unit and in many cases to other core skills and vocational units. Examples at this level include producing a newsletter incorporating text, picture and a table of figures; creating a questionnaire and using a database or spreadsheet to enter and process the information collected, leading to graphs and tables to show survey results; producing a poster, publicity material and a personalised mailshot for a fund-raising event, together with a database of helpers and the kinds of help offered.

Level 2 Specification

Element 2.4: Evaluate the use of information technology

PERFORMANCE CRITERIA

A student must:

PC1 **explain** the **reasons** for using information technology

PC2 **compare** the **methods** used by the student and by others for preparing, processing and presenting information

PC3 **describe** the **software** facilities used to meet the requirements of the **task**

PC4 explain the effects on users of **problems** that can occur when using information technology

PC5 explain the importance of **working safely** and in line with good **working practices**

RANGE

Compare: in terms of speed, ease of use, effort, accuracy

Methods: manual, alternative ways of using information technology

Problems: errors, equipment faults, loss of information

Working safely: safety of the user, safety of the equipment, safety of the information

Software facilities (PC3) these are the tools, operations and methods provided by the software to support the preparation, processing and presentation of information covered in Elements 2.1 to 2.3.

Working practices (PC5) examples include lists of Do's and Don'ts such as keeping cables tidy, positioning screens to avoid reflections, keeping drinks away from equipment, storing disks away from heat and electrical equipment. They also include precautions to avoid loss or corruption of information and unauthorised use of information.

Errors (PC4 range) for example, inaccurate information, inappropriate processing.

Equipment faults (PC4 range) for example, those caused by poorly connected cables, equipment being switched off or wrongly set up, equipment failing.

	Practice Activity	Evidence Opportunity
PC1	6, 7, 11, 15	5, 8, 11
PC2	9, 11	7, 11
PC3	3, 7, 11, 15	7, 8, 11
PC4	11	1, 11
PC5	8	8

Software (PC2) for text, an example is word processing; for graphics, examples are drawing software and painting software; for number work, examples are spreadsheet software and accounts software. Databases could be used to cover both textual and numerical information; desktop publishing could be used to cover both textual and graphical elements.

Easy to edit (PC2 range) this includes, for example, the appropriate use of returns and tabs, and the use of a suitable numerical format when numbers are used for calculation.

Information developed during input (PC1 range) this is information which does not exist in hard-copy form before input, but is put together during the process of input, for example formulas, drawings, ideas or a letter to be drafted.

Graphics (PC1 range) this includes, for example, pictures, photographs, drawings and scanned images, stored digitally, as well as the software tools for creating new images.

Errors (PC2 range) examples include typing mistakes that can be corrected before the return key is pressed. Other examples are an attempt to input a word instead of a date, or to input a number that is too big.

Database structures (PC5 range) the database structure includes input screens with field sizes and types which may be automatically checked when information is entered.

Level 3 Specification

Element 3.1: Prepare Information

PERFORMANCE CRITERIA

A student must:

PC1 select information appropriate to the task

PC2 enter information into **software** in ways that will make it easy to edit

PC3 keep source information required for the task

PC4 store input systematically and make backup copies

PC5 configure software to aid input of **information**

RANGE

Select: information taken from existing sources, information developed during input

Information: text, graphics, numbers

Enter: inputting source information accurately, making immediate corrections to errors noticed on entry, putting right simple equipment faults, using manuals and on-line help facilities, asking for help as appropriate

Software: for text, for graphics, for numbers

Store input systematically: naming files sensibly to indicate the contents, locating files conveniently for subsequent use, creating and using directories to group related files, saving work before and after important changes, saving work before and after important changes, saving work when all the information has been input

Configure software: creating style sheets for text input, creating spreadsheet templates, creating database structures.

Tasks (PC1 and PC3) these are activities which are relevant to the settings in which the student is working and where the use of information technology is judged by the student to be necessary or helpful. They will usually involve work which relates to the requirements of all of the elements in the unit and in many cases to other core skills and vocational units. Examples at this level include producing, with the aid of automated routines, a newsletter incorporating information from a variety of sources and showing evidence of design intended to match the audience and achieve maximum impact; creating a questionnaire and using a database or spreadsheet to enter and analyse the information collected, leading to a report incorporating graphs and tables; producing a poster, publicity material and a personalised mailshot for a fund-raising event, together with a database or spreadsheet to assist planning and management of the event by scheduling activities, keeping track of helpers and accounting for expenditure and income.

Existing sources (PC1 range) examples include printed documents such as price lists of catalogues containing information to go into a database, or images to be scanned. Other examples may be written in longhand, such as notes of a meeting to be word-processed or readings from a survey or experiment that need to go into a spreadsheet.

Simple equipment faults (PC2 range) for example, those caused by poorly connected cables, equipment being switched off or wrongly set up.

Style sheets (PC5 range) these are structures which provide a standard layout, for example, a memo form for use in word processing.

Spreadsheet templates (PC5 range) these are spreadsheets which can be used repeatedly whereby the structure is retained but some information is altered; examples include invoices and order forms.

	Practice Activity	Evidence Opportunity
PC1	2, 3, 4, 5, 6, 7, 9, 10, 13, 16	2, 3, 4, 5, 6, 7, 8, 10, 11, 12
PC2	2, 3, 4, 5, 6, 9, 13, 16	5, 6, 7, 8, 11, 12
PC3	4, 5, 6, 13, 16	5, 7, 12
PC4	5, 13	4, 6, 10
PC5	5, 10, 13, 16	5, 6, 7, 10, 12

Software (PC2 and PC3) for text, an example is word processing; for graphics, examples are drawing software and painting software; for number work, examples are spreadsheet software and accounts software. Databases could be used to cover both textual and numerical information; desktop publishing could be used to cover both textual and graphical elements. CD-ROM software could be used to provide textual, graphical and numerical information.

Resolving differences of format (PC6) the imported material should look natural in its new location. Examples of differences include different fonts, margins, tab settings, paragraph layouts, sizes and/or shapes of graphics, forms of tables, formats of numbers.

Remote sources (PC1 range) these include information held on other computers, accessed via a network or by telecommunication.

Absolute and relative references (PC3 range) an example is the processing of an order, where the cost of the items in any particular row of the spreadsheet is calculated as the unit cost of the item (relative reference, because it relates to this item) times the number of items ordered (another relative reference) increased by the VAT rate (absolute reference to the cell where the current rate for the relevant class of items is stored).

Sorting (PC4 range) for example, sorting records in a database or rows in a spreadsheet.

Importing (PC6 range) for example, bringing information from another source into the file being processed, pulling a picture from a drawing file into a desktop-published file of text, using electronic mail to download information into a file.

Level 3 Specification

Element 3.2: Process information

PERFORMANCE CRITERIA

A student must:

PC1 **find information** required for the task

PC2 use appropriate **software** to **edit information**

PC3 process numerical **information** by using **software** to **make calculations**

PC4 **reorganise information** as required for the task

PC5 save work at **appropriate intervals**

PC6 **combine information** from different sources, resolving differences of format

PC7 create automated routines that aid efficient processing of **information**

RANGE

Find: by looking in the right directory, by looking for files with a given name, by searching for information which meets specified criteria, by accessing remote sources

Information: text, graphics, numbers

Software: for text, for graphics, for numbers

Edit: amending, moving reformatting, copying deleting, inserting

Make calculations: by creating totals in databases or spreadsheets, by using formulas incorporating absolute and relative references to spreadsheet cells

Reorganise: sorting, restructuring stored information

Appropriate intervals: before and after important changes, when the processing is complete

Combine: importing information of the same type, importing information of a different type

Tasks (PC1) these are activities which are relevant to the settings in which the student is working and where the use of information technology is judged by the student to be necessary or helpful. They will usually involve work which relates to the requirements of all of the elements in the unit and in many cases to other core skills and vocational units. Examples at this level include producing, with the aid of automated routines, a newsletter incorporating information from a variety of sources and showing evidence of design intended to match the audience and achieve maximum impact; creating a questionnaire and using a database or spreadsheet to enter and analyse the information collected, leading to a report incorporating graphs and tables; producing a poster, publicity material and a personalised mailshot for a fund-raising event, together with a database or spreadsheet to assist planning and management of the event by scheduling activities, keeping track of helpers and accounting for expenditure and income.

Automated routines (PC7) these are tools which allow repetitive sequences of operations to be programmed into single operations, for example macros, batch files, programmable keys and icons, mail merge, database query and report routines.

Specified criteria (PC1 range) the search criteria will be specified by the student to meet the requirements of the task, for example 'sex = female and age <25'.

Reformatting (PC2 range) this includes both operations on individual items, for example underlining a word or converting a number to currency format, and operations concerning larger collections of information for example changing paragraph layout, the style of shading in a diagram, or the sizes of columns in a table.

Restructuring (PC4 range) for example, changing the sequence in which rows or columns in a spreadsheet are organised, reorganising text under headings and subheadings, reorganising information from a database as required for the task.

	Practice Activity	Evidence Opportunity
PC1	3, 5, 6, 10, 12, 14, 16	8, 9, 13
PC2	2, 3, 4, 5, 6, 9, 13, 15, 16	5, 6, 7, 8, 9, 12
PC3	6, 13, 15	5, 7, 10
PC4	5, 6, 7, 10, 12, 13, 15, 16	6, 7, 8, 10, 12, 13
PC5	2, 3, 4, 5, 6, 7, 9, 10, 13, 15, 16	2, 3, 4, 10, 11
PC6	3, 10, 16	7, 12
PC7	10, 13, 15, 16	7, 10, 12

Tasks (PC2) these are activities which are relevant to the settings in which the student is working and where the use of information technology is judged by the student to be necessary or helpful. They will usually involve work which relates to the requirement of all of the elements in the unit and in many cases to other core skills and vocational units. Examples at this level include producing, with the aid of automated routines, a newsletter incorporating information from a variety of sources and showing evidence of design intended to match the audience and achieve maximum impact; creating a questionnaire and using a database or spreadsheet to enter and analyse the information collected, leading to a report incorporating graphs and tables; producing a poster, publicity material and a personalised mailshot for a fund-raising event, together with a database or spreadsheet to assist planning and management of the event by scheduling activities, keeping track of helpers and accounting for expenditure and income.

Software (PC3 and PC4) for text, an example is word processing; for graphics examples are drawing software and painting software; for number work, examples are spreadsheet software and accounts software. Databases could be used to cover both textual and numerical information; desktop publishing could be used to cover both textual and graphical elements.

Combined information (PC5) this is information in the form of text, graphics and number combined into a consistent format.

Level 3 Specification

Element 3.3: Present information

PERFORMANCE CRITERIA

A student must:

PC1 **prepare information** for presentation

PC2 present **information** in different ways and select which way best meets the **requirements** of the task

PC3 use appropriate **software** to display **information**

PC4 use appropriate **software** to produce hard copy of **information**

PC5 present combined **information** in a consistent format

PC6 store **information** in files and make backup copies

RANGE

Prepare: selecting the form and content of the information to match the requirement of the task, date-stamping and paginating documents, using named directories for associated display files, storing successive developments of information for presentation with version numbers and informative file names.

Information: text, graphics, numbers

Requirements: fitness for purpose, matched to audience, clarity, accuracy, consistent format

Software: for text, graphics, numbers

Consistent format (PC5) screen display and print-out should be designed so that the information is clear and is arranged in manageable portions. There should be no output across page breaks or perforations of continuous stationery and tables should be easy to read.

Backup copies (PC6) work saved on a separate storage medium, for example, a floppy disk.

Selecting (PC1 range) the form and content of the information to be presented requires the application of design skills, taking into account for example the desired impact of the product, the appropriate balance of 'white space' with text, tables and illustrations, the logical presentation of information, as well as more detailed aspects of layout.

Version numbers (PC1 range) examples include automated version numbering systems for file names or the use of names like P1C1 and P1C2 which help to show the sequence of development of a drawing.

File names (PC1 range) as far as possible, file names should convey information about the content and purpose of the file.

	Practice Activity	Evidence Opportunity
PC1	14, 15, 16	6, 8, 10, 11, 14
PC2	3, 7, 10, 13, 15, 16	4, 7, 8, 10, 12
PC3	2, 3, 4, 5, 6, 7, 9, 10, 13, 15, 16	2, 5, 6, 9, 12
PC4	2, 3, 4, 5, 6, 7, 9, 10, 13, 15, 16	2, 3, 4, 5, 6, 7, 8, 10, 11, 12
PC5	3, 10, 16	8, 12
PC6	5, 10, 12, 16	6, 12, 13

Tasks (PC4) these are activities which are relevant to the settings in which the student is working and where the use of information technology is judged by the student to be necessary or helpful. They will usually involve work which relates to the requirement of all of the elements in the unit and in many cases to other core skills and vocational units. Examples at this level include producing, with the aid of automated routines, a newsletter incorporating information from a variety of sources and showing evidence of design intended to match the audience and achieve maximum impact; creating a questionnaire and using a database or spreadsheet to enter and analyse the information collected, leading to a report incorporating graphs and tables; producing a poster, publicity material and a personalised mailshot for a fund-raising event, together with a database or spreadsheet to assist planning and management of the event by scheduling activities, keeping track of helpers and accounting for expenditure and income.

Effectiveness (PC3 range) the effectiveness of a system includes, for example, the extent to which it meets a perceived need, offers new or improved ways of using information is 'user-friendly' and is integrated within the wider context.

System faults (PC5 range) these are to do with mismatches between the design of the system and what it is required to do; examples of faults in major systems feature regularly in the press and provide a useful source for learning.

Level 3 Specification

Element 3.4: Evaluate the use of information technology

PERFORMANCE CRITERIA

A student must:

PC1 **explain** and justify the **reasons** for using information technology

PC2 **compare** the **methods** used by the student and by others for preparing, processing and presenting information

PC3 **evaluate** alternative **systems** for managing information

PC4 describe the software facilities used to meet the requirements of the task

PC5 explain the effects on users of **problems** that can occur when using information technology

PC6 explain the importance of **working safely** and in line with good working practices

RANGE

Compare: in terms of speed, ease of use, effort, accuracy

Methods: manual, alternative ways of using information technology

Evaluate: effectiveness, cost, effects on employment, benefits (to individuals, to organisations) disadvantages (to individuals, to organisations)

Systems: manual, information technology

Problems: system faults, errors, equipment faults, loss of information

Working safely: safety of the user, safety of the equipment, safety of the information

Reasons (PC1) examples include making things more effective or easier when processing a large volume of information, when undertaking an activity which will take a long time to perform manually, or when storing large amounts of information.

Systems (PC3) evaluating a system includes considering the purpose and the effects of using information technology within the wider context of the application, as well as examining the way the system works.

Software facilities (PC4) these are the tools, operations and methods provided by the software to support the preparation, processing and presentation of information covered in Elements 3.1 to 3.3.

Working practices (PC6) examples include lists of Do's and Don'ts such as keeping cables tidy, positioning screens to avoid reflections, keeping drinks away from equipment, storing disks away from heat and electrical equipment. They also include precautions to avoid loss or corruption of information and unauthorised use of information, the prevention or detection and removal of viruses, and a proper respect for copyright of software.

Individuals and organisations (PC3 range) there is a contrast between the views of the organisation, of the users of the services provided by the organisation, and of others. An important consideration is proper control of the use of sensitive information, an area where data protection legislation applies.

Errors (PC5 range) for example, inaccurate information, inappropriate processing, failure of software to deal with exceptional situations.

Equipment faults (PC5 range) for example, those caused by poorly connected cables, equipment being switched off or wrongly set up, equipment failing.

	Practice Activity	Evidence Opportunity
PC1	6, 7, 11, 15	7, 8, 11
PC2	9, 11	11
PC3	11	6, 11
PC4	3, 7, 11, 15	7, 8, 11
PC5	11	1, 11
PC6	8	6

PRACTICE ACTIVITIES

The setting

The Remedy group comprises a small chain of five shops which sell a range of pharmaceutical, baby care and health and beauty products. Each shop is located in a town centre shopping precinct. The company is based in Kent. The five shops are in Folkestone, Canterbury, Dover, Ashford and Maidstone. The company Head Office is in Folkestone. The company plays an active role in the community, primarily developing products which are 'environmentally friendly' by supporting charitable schemes and recycling waste materials from its retailing enterprise.

The activities in this book are based on the work roles that staff and volunteers carry out at Remedy. This text will focus on Remedy's Head Office and on the Remedy shop in Dover. You will be introduced to four key people: Eileen MacQuarry, Gurdip Bola, Judith Argyle and Clare Delaney. Eileen founded the company and is the owner and the Managing Director. She has one assistant working for her in the office. Her name is Gurdip Bola and she is being trained for management. Gurdip goes to college one day a week where she is doing a GNVQ in Management. Judith Argyle is the manager of the Dover shop. The Assistant Manager is called Clare Delaney. All of these people use Information Technology in one way or another.

Information Technology (IT) is used to gather and process information. This helps organisations such as Remedy in their administration and management. All of the shops have computers and there is also a computer at Head Office. As yet, the computers are not connected to each other, but Eileen MacQuarry wants to link them. She has just connected her computer to the Internet System which means that, using her computer, she can communicate with other people all over the world and access vast amounts of information.

Eileen MacQuarry
*Managing
Director*

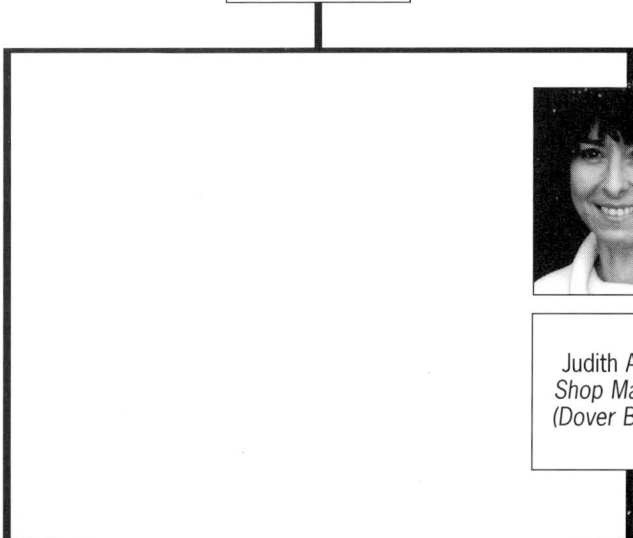

Judith Argyle
*Shop Manager
(Dover Branch)*

Gurdip Bola
*Assistant to the
Managing
Director and
trainee manager*

Clare Delaney
*Assistant
Manager
(Dover Branch)*

1   Logging problems, errors and faults

When staff at the Remedy shops use the computer systems, they inevitably encounter a number of errors and faults. Some of these errors may be due to the hardware or the software that is used. Others may be the fault of the user (perhaps because little guidance is available to them in the office). Many problems stem from simple errors, such as:

● the wrong key being pressed;
● the required disk not being in the disk drive;
● the printer being off-line.

Whatever the cause of the problem, it is important to keep track of it and to learn from it.

Gurdip Bola works at Remedy Head Office as a trainee manager. She attends college one day a week, where she is taking a GNVQ Management course. As she is learning how to use computers at college, she does a lot of work on the computer at Head Office. When Gurdip comes across problems, she uses a special Head Office form to keep a record of what they are and how she deals with them. Keeping such a record helps both Gurdip and others who work for Remedy to diagnose the causes of future faults, and thereby possibly to prevent them from happening again.

You too need to keep a record of how you deal with errors and faults in your working environment. This will help you to develop your IT skills and provide a record for your assessment portfolio.

Here are some examples of the entries that Gurdip has made.

Problem	Date	Action Taken and Comments
Keyboard not working	9/12/96	Checked keyboard connecting lead. It was loose at the back. Made sure it was connected securely.
'Disk faulty' message	12/12/96	Marked Disk 'damaged' – got another, which worked fine.
Database program crashed	12/12/96	Wrote down error message and called Jane.
Disk files accidently deleted	12/12/96	Looked for back-ups – couldn't find them. Talked to Eileen. She has now installed a password system to stop 'tampering'. Agreed we should also have a back-up system
Database program crashed	12/12/96	Ran the virus check. Hard disk appeared to be OK. Wrote down error message and informed Eileen.

The first thing you have to think about is how you are going to record your errors. You could use separate forms, like the ones used at Remedy Head Office, or you could keep an 'error-logging' book so that you can ensure that all records of errors are kept together.

EVIDENCE

Either keep an 'error-logging' book or use the form on page 90 to record any problems that you come across when working on the computer. Maintain this record over as long a period as possible and submit it with your evidence portfolio.

2 Preparing notes for Remedy shop managers

As part of her responsibilities in the running of Remedy Head Office, Eileen MacQuarry, the Managing Director, has to prepare a letter to be sent to all the Branch Managers of the five Remedy shops, explaining the health and beauty franchise that is going to be introduced in all the stores. Eileen also intends to outline the new sales and returns procedures related to these changes. She asks Gurdip to prepare the document.

The IT skills Gurdip will use to do this include:

▶ word-processing notes that have been written by hand;
▶ checking the text that she has keyed in for mistakes;
▶ saving the text;
▶ printing the text.

You can practise these skills by following the steps that Gurdip takes and carrying out the equivalent processes on your own computer.

Practise

1. Checking the source document

First of all, Gurdip reads her original, hand-written document and checks it for clarity and accuracy. This is Gurdip's source document (you could use it for your own practice).

> HEALTH AND BEAUTY PARTNERSHIP WITH OASIS
>
> At the last managers' meeting it was agreed to invite external franchise operators to submit tenders for setting up their franchise operations within each of our stores. I am pleased to report that Oasis have been sucessful in attaining the franchise and they expect to commence "moving in" as soon as is practical. All their products are made from natural ingredients, without chemical additives, and the products are not tested on animals. As many of you may know, up till

now they have confined their sales to mail order, and the occasional craft fair. All their packaging has been in brown wrapping paper. Oasis is now trying to expand by setting up outlets in approved shops and it is going to up its profile. Their range of health and beauty products will be sold initially at our Dover shop, under their "Oasis" brand names, however the overall scheme will be marketed under our name.

We will be monitoring this operation very closely and are aware that sales of their products might detract from our own brands. It is a distinct possibility that Oasis will add some of our products to their list and they will be marketed under the Oasis label.

In the meantime we will carefully monitor the sales of the Oasis products, in order to see if they do attract custom and to see how they affect the sales of our own brands.

The integrated program which Gurdip selects

2. Choosing the application

Next, Gurdip needs to decide what software application to use. She doesn't use a typewriter because it would not be possible to change any mistakes in the text or the layout without having to key the whole document again. Her task is to present text, so she chooses a suite of programs which includes a word-processing option.

You could use a word-processing or a desktop publishing program instead. All of these applications let you view the text on the screen and make any changes before you print it.

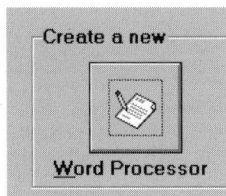

3. Entering the word-processing program

The word-processing program which all the staff use is shown on Gurdip's computer screen as an icon. When she clicks on the icon she automatically gets into the program. From this she selects the word-processing option.

You may not be presented with an on-screen menu to choose from – if this is the case you may have to key in commands to start up the program.

Most word-processing programs take you into a layout where you can start keying text immediately. Some, however, will require you to open a new document first. Other programs will ask you to name your document before you enter text. The name you give your document should reflect its purpose (in this case 'FRANCH1' would be an appropriate name).

HELP
If you need help in naming files, turn to page 107.

4. Keying in the text

When the cursor (the flashing marker on the screen) appears in the top left-hand corner of the screen, Gurdip begins to key in her text. As she

Guidance

On a typewriter you have to press the carriage return at the end of every line to take you to the beginning of the next line. The equivalent of the carriage return on a keyboard is commonly known as the ENTER key. However, word-processing programs have a 'word wrap' facility which automatically judges whether a word will fit in on the line. If a word will not fit, it will automatically be forced over on to the next line. So, when keying in continuous text on a word processor, you mustn't use the ENTER key at the end of a line. This should only be done when you specifically want to advance on to a new line (e.g. to create a new paragraph).

Guidance

Many people use the backspace key to delete. This may be found above the ENTER key. This deletes the character immediately to the left of the cursor.

Guidance

Make sure every word is separated by a space. Space is crucial in word processing because it is the way that the program recognises separate words. Spaces also affect functions like word wrapping and word count. Always include spaces after full stops and commas. Some people suggest that full stops are followed by two spaces, especially in letters, while others argue for one space. Use whichever you, or your organisation, prefer, and stick to it so that your work is consistent.

presses a character key on her keyboard, that character appears on the screen and the cursor moves to where the next character will appear.

Unavoidably, mistakes are made as text is keyed in. Often, words and characters will need to be deleted. To do this, Gurdip uses the arrows on her keypad to move the cursor over the mistake and then presses the delete key. This, however, can be a rather slow process, as only one character is deleted at a time. If Gurdip wants to delete more than one character, she can select the text she wants to delete and 'block' it ('blocked' text is usually shown highlighted on screen). When the delete key is pressed after text has been blocked, all the text in the block is deleted.

"Oasis" brand names, however the overall scheme will be marketed under our name

We will be monitoring this operation very closely and are aware that sales of their products might detract from our own brands. It is a distinct possibility that will allow Oasis to add some of our products to their list and they will be marketed under the Oasis label.

In the meantime we will carefully monitor the sales of the Oasis products, in order to see if it does attract custom and to see how it affects the sales of our own brand

Text which has been highlighted on screen

Some systems can use a mouse to relocate the cursor. To move to a new position on screen using a mouse, move the pointer to the new position and click the left button. You can block text using a mouse by clicking and keeping your finger down while you 'drag' the pointer to the end of the text you want to delete.

As there are different delete keys, and more than one way to delete, it is suggested that you experiment.

While she is keying in, Gurdip notices that she sometimes misses text out, which she needs to go back and insert. When this happens, she moves the cursor to the relevant position and keys in the missing text. When you do this, you may find that you are keying over existing text. If this does happen, you are in 'overwrite' mode (i.e. the text that you key in will *replace* the existing text, so you will lose it) and you should switch to 'insert' mode (i.e. the text you key in will be *added* where you have positioned the cursor). Find the INSERT/OVERWRITE key and press it. You should now be in insert mode. There will be a status line somewhere on the screen that will tell you what mode you are in.

| Col 1 | | 3:14 PM | REC | MRK | EXT | OVR | |

OVR on this status line indicates that the program is in the overwrite mode.

Another problem which you may come across is when the text you key in all appears in capital letters (i.e. in upper case). This happens when the CAPS LOCK key is on. There is usually an illuminated indicator on the keyboard which tells you if this key is on. (Many programs also display a CAPS

LOCK indicator on the screen.) Pressing the CAPS LOCK key switches from on to off, and vice versa.

5. Checking mistakes and spelling

Mistakes can go unnoticed while text is being keyed in. To ensure that there are no keying errors or spelling mistakes in her document, Gurdip uses the spell-check function that the word-processing program provides. She finds that there are some words that the spell-check function does not recognise (e.g. 'sucessful'). When spell-checkers come across words that they do not recognise, they highlight them and give you the opportunity to change them. They also often suggest alternatives. When Gurdip's spell-checker highlights the word 'sucessful', one of the suggestions it provides is 'successful' (see below). Gurdip chooses to change her mis-keyed word to 'successful' and the program automatically corrects her mistake and continues with the spell-check.

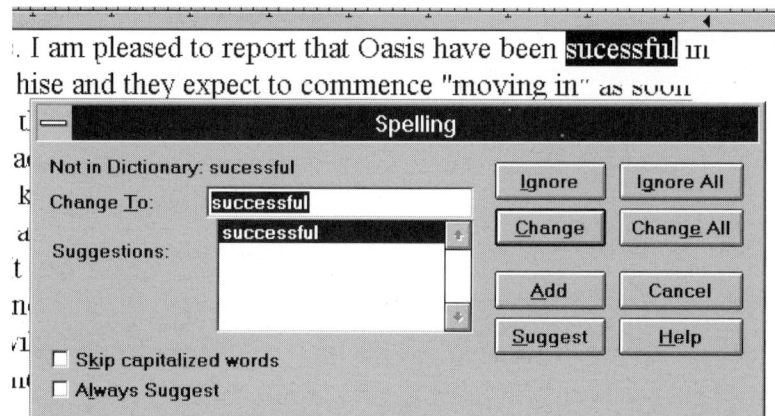

I am pleased to report that Oasis have been **sucessful** in hise and they expect to commence "moving in" as soon

Spelling

Not in Dictionary: sucessful

Change To: successful

Suggestions: successful

☐ Skip capitalized words
☐ Always Suggest

Ignore | Ignore All
Change | Change All
Add | Cancel
Suggest | Help

Note how the spell-checker can suggest alternatives

When the spell-checker does not recognise a word, it offers the option of adding the 'new' word to the dictionary. However, do resist adding new words until you are more familiar with the program and the requirements of other users. If you add to the dictionary, the dictionary will change for all the users of that computer, and there is a danger that words you add will be identical to other, misspelt, words which will not then be caught by the spell-checker.

6. Checking the whole document

After running the spell-checker, Gurdip re-reads the whole document. You should always read through your text on screen and compare it with the source document. You will probably find more mistakes, in which case you will need to move around within the document and insert and delete as necessary.

If you cannot see all the text you have keyed in on the screen, you can use the directional arrows or press the PAGE UP/PAGE DOWN keys. If the word-processing program uses *Windows*, you can click the mouse pointer on the arrows at the right-hand corners of the window frame to move around the document.

Guidance

You should check against your source information and retain this source document until you are sure it will not be needed.

HELP
If you need help with *Windows*, turn to page 116.

```
File  Edit  View  Insert  Format  Tools  Table  Wi
New...                                      Ctrl+N
Open...                                     Ctrl+O
Close
Save                                        Ctrl+S
Save As...
Save All
Find File...
Summary Info...
Templates...
Page Setup...
Print Preview
Print...                                    Ctrl+P
```

The options available under the FILE menu vary from program to program

---

Guidance

If you have a preview facility, do use it before you print, as it can avoid waste of paper. (You will be able to see, for instance, if your document goes over the page length by just one line.)

? **HELP**
If you need help with naming files, turn to page 107.
If you need help with directories, turn to page 107.

Guidance

It is bad practice to turn the computer off while you are still in the program – you may lose your data. Also, because programs sometimes use temporary files which are only deleted when shutting down in the recommended manner, you could clutter up your directories unnecessarily if you do not exit the program properly.

---

7. Printing the document

Once she is happy that there are no errors in the document she has created on screen, Gurdip selects the PRINT option (in *Windows*-based programs this is found in the FILE menu). This brings up the print menu. Before actually printing the document, however, Gurdip selects a preview option from the print menu. This allows her to see how the text will be laid out on paper.

After previewing her document, Gurdip checks that the printer is 'on-line' (i.e. turned on and connected to the computer) and has paper in it. She then selects the PRINT command from the print menu to print out a hard copy of the document.

Always check your printed version for errors. Many people find it easier to spot errors on printed copy than on the screen, but do also get into the habit of checking on screen first, to avoid wasting paper.

8. Saving the document

Gurdip's program automatically gave her document a default name before she keyed in any text. In order to store what she has created on screen, so that she can access it again, Gurdip has to save her document under a new name. (In *Windows*-based programs the SAVE option is found in the FILE menu.) Gurdip chooses the SAVE AS option, and is asked to give her document a name. When you save your document, it is important to give it a name that reflects the purpose of the document so that you will be able to find it again easily. (Gurdip calls hers 'FRANCH1'.) Unless you choose to save your file in a different directory, it will be saved in your current directory (i.e. the directory that you are working in at the time you save the document).

9. Leaving the word-processing program

Once Gurdip has saved her document with a filename, she leaves the word-processing program by choosing the EXIT option from the FILE menu. There are various ways of exiting different programs – a common way is by pressing the ESCAPE key repeatedly. If the method of exiting your program is not obvious, use your computer's HELP menu or seek help from somebody else.

EVIDENCE
Assignments 4 and 5 (page 92) provide opportunities to produce evidence of achievement in inputting and presenting textual information.

3 Publicising a new range of products

Notices are used to communicate information to customers at all branches of Remedy. Eileen MacQuarry, the Managing Director, wants an A4 notice, announcing the new health and beauty franchise, to be displayed on the notice board of the Dover shop where they will be trialing a franchise with Oasis. The notice needs to be eye-catching, with clear text that is legible and easy to read.

This is the draft notice that Eileen has sketched out for Gurdip to follow.

The IT skills Gurdip will use to produce this notice include:

▶ entering data;
▶ formatting the text for readability;
▶ aligning the text;
▶ importing the logo into her document;
▶ saving and printing the final version.

You can practise these skills by following the steps that Gurdip takes and carrying out the equivalent processes on your own computer.

Practise

1. Choosing the application

Gurdip does not have access to a sophisticated program at Head Office. However, the word-processing package that she can access (which is called *Write* – a free program provided with *Windows*) offers a wide range of fonts and text layout and is capable of importing images from other applications.

HELP
For more information about desktop publishing, turn to page 103. For an explanation of an integrated package, turn to page 104.

Guidance

Desktop publishing programs tend to allow the user much more control over page layout.

Guidance

In *Windows* 95 *Write* is known as *Wordpad*.

This type of application used to be called desktop publishing. However, most modern word-processing software is powerful enough to carry out all that is necessary to produce the notice. Depending on the software available to you, when you practise this activity you could use:

- word-processing software, as long as it is able offer a variety of fonts and import graphics images;
- a desktop publishing program;
- an integrated package which offers a variety of fonts and can import images;
- a drawing program.

Whatever package you do use, it is likely that you will use a mouse and work in a *Windows*-like environment.

2. Opening the document and entering text

Gurdip enters *Write* from a menu on her screen. Once she gets into the application she can start keying in the text for the notice straightaway. Some programs will require you to open a new document first.

3. Centring the text

To position all the text in the centre of the page, Gurdip highlights it using the mouse and chooses the PARAGRAPH pull-down menu (see below/left). She then chooses the CENTRED option and the highlighted text is automatically centred.

Choosing the centre align icon from the tool bar will centre the highlighted text

Different programs use different ways of centring. Sometimes highlighted text can be centred by means of hitting special keys or a combination of keys. Alternatively, on your package centring may be done through a FORMAT menu, within which there is a PARAGRAPH option.

4. Applying a font

From the FORMAT menu, Gurdip selects CHARACTER and then the FONTS option which brings up a list of fonts (see below). She chooses a font called Arial. This is a plain sans-serif font that will stand out well at a distance. She fixes the typesize at 24 points.

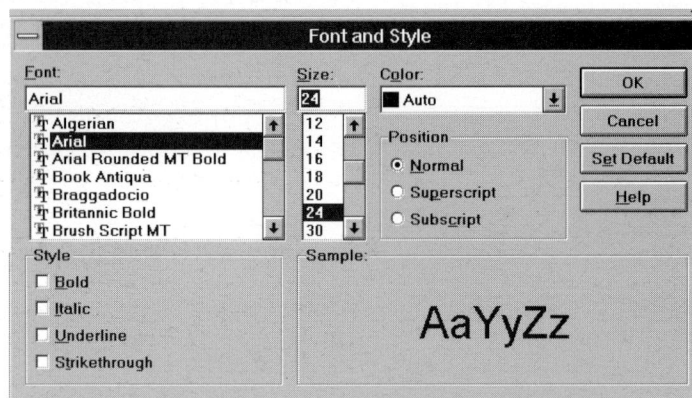

Altering the font and font size

You may have to follow a different route to select fonts in the package you use. For instance, CHARACTER may be an option within a FORMAT menu, or the name of the selected font may be displayed below a menu bar, where you can change it. Find out where your font choices are. When you select one, bear in mind that the notice needs to be easily legible.

5. Importing the logo

Gurdip needs to incorporate the Remedy logo into her document. The logo has already been drawn and saved on the computer as a separate file so that it can be incorporated in all kinds of Remedy documents.

First, she positions her cursor above the text. She then selects the INSERT OBJECT option from the EDIT pull-down menu (see left). This enables her to retrieve the logo into her document. Once it has been retrieved, Gurdip is able to move it and size it, again using the EDIT menu.

Obviously, you will not have a logo ready made for you, but you may be able to retrieve appropriate ready-made images from Clipart directories, through the INSERT option or another menu on the package you are using.

Another method of retrieving an image is to enter the application in which it was created, COPY it (using an EDIT menu), return to the application where you have keyed in the text and activate the PASTE facility at the point where you want the picture to be inserted.

You might wish to highlight the whole notice by drawing a border around the edge of it, or just the picture. Find out if this is possible with your program.

6. Printing the notice

If it is possible, preview your notice on screen. This enables you to see what it will look like when it is printed out. When previewing the document Gurdip decided that it would look better displayed in landscape format.

Guidance

One of the core skills requirements is to display information on screen.

New Health and Beauty Franchise!

**Remedy LTD is pleased to announce that
OASIS HEALTH & BEAUTY PRODUCTS LTD**

**have been appointed the
Health and Beauty franchise
operators in the Dover branch.**

**Remedy will be keeping you informed
of new developments and special offers.**

Here is Gurdip's notice, printed out.

When you are satisfied with its appearance, print a copy of your notice.

7. Saving the file and exiting

When she is happy with the printed notice, Gurdip saves her notice as a file called NOTICE1 and exits the program.

Remember to save your file with an appropriate name before you exit from the program.

8. Appraising the notice

Gurdip shows the result of her efforts to Eileen MacQuarry, who agrees that the notice is very effective and that it is not necessary to use expensive dedicated drawing or desktop publishing programs to achieve striking results.

EVIDENCE
Assignment 4 provides an opportunity to produce evidence of achievement in combining text and images and manipulating fonts.

> ### Guidance
>
> If you have any problems, e.g. with printing, remember to fill in your log sheet. See page 16.

> ### Guidance
>
> This will help you to contribute to the LEVEL 2 requirement to 'explain the reasons for using information technology'.

4   Preparing a letter to all sales staff

An opportunity exists to expand the D&P (developing and processing) operation within each of the shops. Photon, a photographic developing and processing company (referred to in business circles as 'photofinishers') has approached Remedy with a photofinishing service that significantly undercuts the cost of the local competitors. Eileen MacQuarry, has drafted the following letter, to be sent to all sales staff, for Gurdip Bola to produce on the computer.

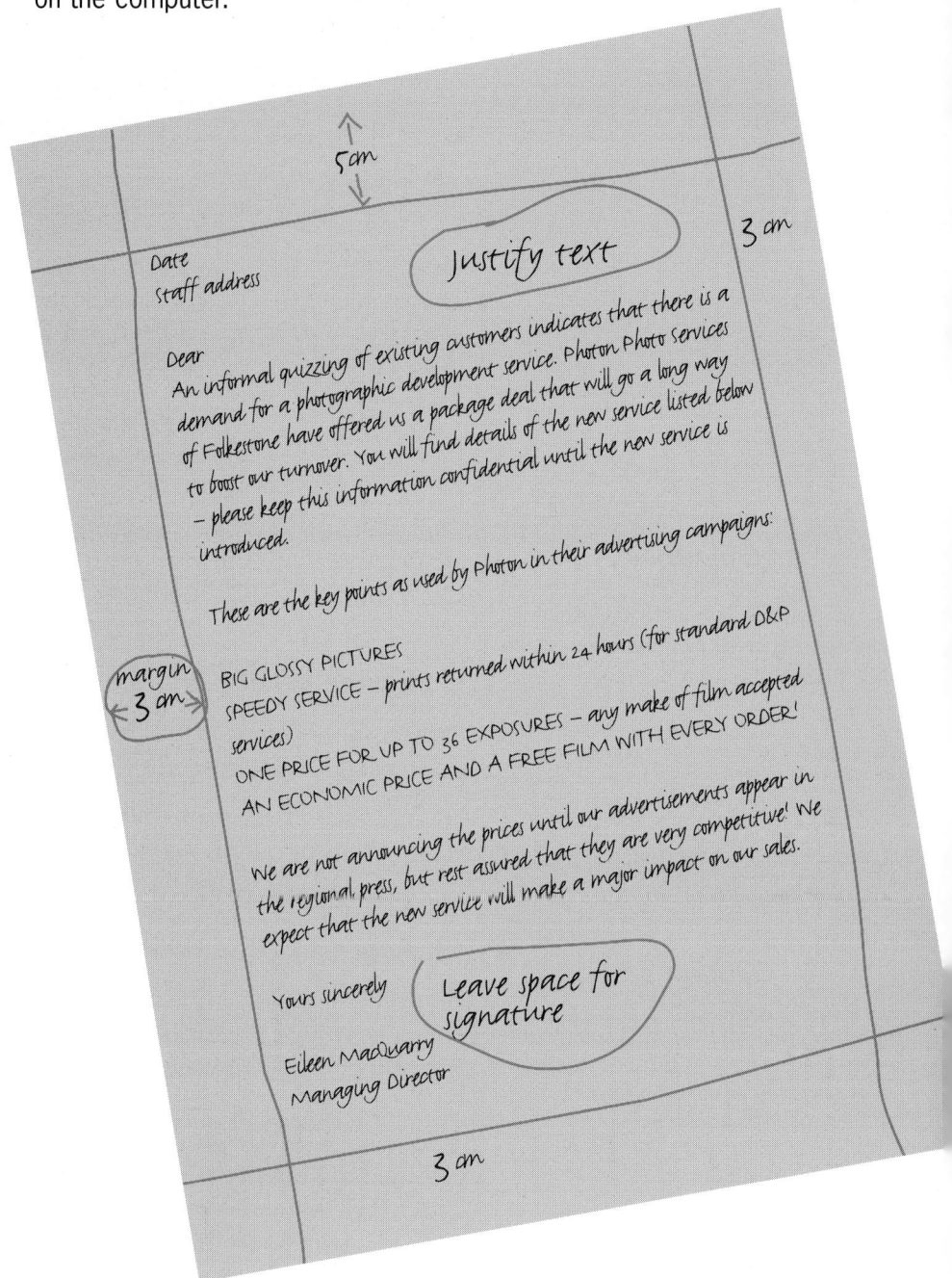

5cm

3 cm

Date
Staff address

Justify text

Dear

An informal quizzing of existing customers indicates that there is a demand for a photographic development service. Photon Photo Services of Folkestone have offered us a package deal that will go a long way to boost our turnover. You will find details of the new service listed below — please keep this information confidential until the new service is introduced.

These are the key points as used by Photon in their advertising campaigns:

margin
3 cm

BIG GLOSSY PICTURES
SPEEDY SERVICE — prints returned within 24 hours (for standard D&P services)
ONE PRICE FOR UP TO 36 EXPOSURES — any make of film accepted
AN ECONOMIC PRICE AND A FREE FILM WITH EVERY ORDER!

We are not announcing the prices until our advertisements appear in the regional press, but rest assured that they are very competitive! We expect that the new service will make a major impact on our sales.

Yours sincerely

Leave space for signature

Eileen MacQuarry
Managing Director

3 cm

The IT skills Gurdip will use include:

▶ inputting and formatting the above draft text;
▶ checking the text for mistakes;
▶ printing the text;
▶ saving the text.

You can practise these skills by following the steps that Gurdip takes and carrying out the equivalent processes on your own computer.

Practise

HELP
If you need help with naming files, turn to page 107.

1. Choosing the application

The first decision Gurdip has to make is what software application to use. As the main purpose of the task is to present text, a word-processing program will be adequate.

2. Entering the word-processing program and keying the text

The installed word-processing program is shown on Gurdip's screen as an icon. You may need to select a menu option or key in commands to start up the program.

It may be necessary for you to name your document before you start keying in text. If so, the name you give it should reflect the purpose of the document.

Most word-processing programs take you into a layout where you can start keying text immediately.

Use Gurdip's source document to practise keying in text.

3. Checking the whole document

Once Gurdip has keyed in all the text on screen, she reads it through and compares it with the source document.

When you check your document, you will probably find mistakes. If your word processor has a spell-check function, you should use it to check for keying errors and spelling mistakes.

4. Saving the draft

To save her document, Gurdip chooses the SAVE AS option from the FILE menu. She calls it PHOTON1. If you are asked to give your document a name at this stage, remember that it should reflect the document's purpose.

5. Formatting the text

Gurdip will be printing the letter out on headed paper, like this.

REMEDY

Head Office
19 Market Place
Folkestone NA19 6WE
Tel: 01303 29751
Fax: 01303 29783

Guidance

There are many different ways of leaving space for letterheads. You could increase the measurement of the top margin by selecting an option from a FORMAT menu. If you find that you are doing this regularly, it is probably worthwhile using a pre-designed letter template (see page 56 for an example of a template).

There has to be enough room for the Remedy logo before the text starts, so Gurdip measures how much room it will take up on the headed paper. She decides to leave 5 cm at the top so that her text will not be printed across the letterhead, and does this by pressing the carriage return a number of times.

If you are using headed paper, remember to take the heading into account when you are formatting your page.

Remedy Head Office uses a standard layout for all its documents. Gurdip leaves double-line spacing between the date and the salutation (the salutation is the opening part of the letter which greets the reader, i.e. 'Dear'...), and between the salutation and the body of the text. She does this by pressing the ENTER key twice.

The right and left margins (3 cm each) have already been set as a default on Gurdip's computer. You will probably have to set your margins yourself. You may be able to do this from a menu option. If you are using a more powerful text processing program which uses a mouse and provides 'WYSIWYG' (**w**hat **y**ou **s**ee **i**s **w**hat **y**ou **g**et) facilities, an on-screen ruler will be available, and you will be able to change the margin settings by clicking on the margin indicators and dragging them inwards or outwards.

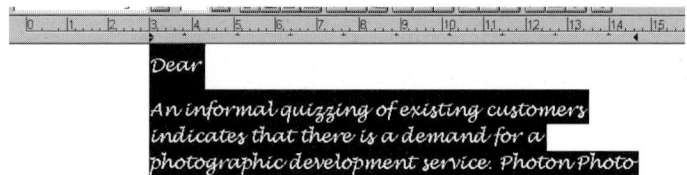

The blocked text on this screen can be aligned by moving the margin indicator arrow which appears under the ruler

Gurdip uses a fully justified format for Remedy Head Office letters (i.e. all the text is lined up in a straight line on the right-hand side as well as on the left-hand side). The program does this by inserting extra spaces between words. Gurdip justifies her text by blocking (i.e. highlighting) it all, selecting the FORMAT menu and choosing the JUSTIFICATION command. You might find that your program uses a PARAGRAPH menu or a WORD ALIGNMENT command, or that JUSTIFY appears as an icon option.

For the close of the letter, a four- or five-line spacing is left between the end of the letter and the name and title of the sender. This leaves space for the signature, e.g.:

Yours sincerely

Eileen MacQuarry

Managing Director

6. Printing the document

Before printing the letter, Gurdip uses the print preview facility on her computer. If you have the ability to preview, do use it because it will show

Guidance

In many programs the PRINT option is found in the FILE menu. If you have any difficulties in printing your letter, try using the program's HELP facilities.

Guidance

In *Windows*-based programs you can shut down by double-clicking the mouse pointer in the top left-hand corner of the relevant window.

? HELP
If you need help with naming files, turn to page 107.
If you need help with directories, turn to page 107.

you how the text will be laid out on paper before you print it, and will help to avoid wasting paper.

Prior to printing, check that the printer is 'on-line' and has paper in it.

7. Saving the document

Gurdip wants to keep the first version of the letter intact, just in case errors occur with subsequent savings. One way of helping you to keep track of different versions of a document is to sequence the file names. For this reason, Gurdip saves it with the name 'PHOTON2'. As she does not specify another directory to save the file to, 'PHOTON2' is saved in Gurdip's current directory. Gurdip also files away the original handwritten draft in case there is a need to check against the original specification later on.

EVIDENCE
Assignment 4 provides an opportunity to produce evidence of achievement in inputting and presenting textual information.

5 Computerising information about staff

The present system for storing information about staff at Head Office is to use filing cards on which information is written rather haphazardly. Often, a lot of time is spent searching for the right card, and cards sometimes get lost.

Gurdip has been given the job of storing this information on computer where it will be of use in the future.

The IT skills Gurdip will use to do this include:

Guidance

'Data' (plural of datum) is the name given to text, numbers or images that you input into your computer. A computer can only process data; it does not understand it. For example the number 250646 stored in a computer is data, but when someone understands it as, for instance, someone's date of birth, it becomes information.

▶ selecting an appropriate package;
▶ setting up a simple database;
▶ entering the information;
▶ saving the information;
▶ checking and editing the information;
▶ searching the information;
▶ sorting the information;
▶ printing a standard report.

You can practise these skills by following the steps that Gurdip takes and carrying out the equivalent processes on your own computer.

1. Data protection

The first thing Gurdip does is to check that it is permissible for Head Office to computerise the data. Data users must comply with the Data Protection Act of 1984, which says that businesses that store information

Practise

about people on computer must register with the Data Protection Registrar and state how the computerised information will be used. Eileen MacQuarry informs Gurdip that Remedy is already registered. All of the staff have agreed to their details being computerised. Gurdip is therefore confident that Remedy Head Office will not be contravening the law.

MARK HARTSHORN, MR   DOVER
21 CHESTNUT CLOSE
BUCKLAND
DOVER DO7 8YV
01304 45345
DATE OF BIRTH   23/03/66

SHIRLEY SQUIRES, MISS   ASHFORD
4 RICHMOND DRIVE
SEVINGTON
ASHFORD AS5 6GF
01233 22213
DATE OF BIRTH   13/09/70

JEF ROBINSON, MR   FOLKESTONE
7 CAMPION RD
CHERITON
FOLKESTONE NA19 6GH
01303 769938
DATE OF BIRTH   22/10/53

JUDITH ARGYLE, MRS   DOVER
99 BARLEY CLOSE
DOVER DO7 1JV
01304 335843
DATE OF BIRTH   29/11/62

ROSEMARY FRASER-HARDY, MISS   CANTERBURY
10 CHAPEL STREET
CANTERBURY KF5 3WE
01227 342251
DATE OF BIRTH   29/11/64

CLARE DELANEY, MS   DOVER
7 CAMPION RD
CHERITON
FOLKESTONE NA19 6GH
01303 769938
DATE OF BIRTH   01/03/61

SUKHINDER KAUSHAL, MISS   FOLKESTONE
43 HALL FARM ROAD
SANDGATE
FOLKESTONE FO3 4RT
01303 35843
DATE OF BIRTH   03/03/78

KEITH LYSENCKO, MR CANTERBURY
57 PARK ROAD
HALES PLACE
CANTERBURY CA5 6TT
01227 988818
DATE OF BIRTH   07/02/69

HARRY DAWE, MR   MAIDSTONE
49 CHESTNUT CLOSE
HINXHILL
MAIDSTONE MA6 3TR
01622 3017482
DATE OF BIRTH   25/06/46

DAVID HUCKER, MR   CANTERBURY
2 AVENUE ROAD
HALES PLACE
CANTERBURY CA5 6TT
01227 34355
DATE OF BIRTH   25/06/38

LINFORD ANDREWS, MR   DOVER
1 MORTIMER DRIVE
BUCKLAND
DOVER WM13 6BH
01304 3678845
DATE OF BIRTH   01/03/62

CATHERINE HINDES, MISS   MAIDSTONE
110 DOVER ROAD
MAIDSTONE MA16 7SR
01622 683721
DATE OF BIRTH   11/01/64

A selection of the cards showing employee details

The data shown on these source cards has been made up, so you do not have to worry about the implications of the Data Protection Act while you are following this activity.

2. Choosing the application

The next decision to be made is what sort of computer application to use. Many people use databases to store details like names and addresses. You

Guidance

This activity provides an introduction to databases. In working through the activity you are required to set up a simple database. Outside of education and training courses the vast majority of users of databases do not set them up. As, quite rightly, there is no requirement at LEVEL 2 for you to set up a database, you can use a database which has already been set up, or you could get somebody to set this one up for you. Whatever you decide to do, it is recommended that you undertake this activity because it is a good way of introducing you to databases and it permits you to do other things with the database, such as use searches, sort data and set up a mailshot (see activity 10). If you need help with databases, turn to page 98.

? HELP
If you need help with understanding fields and field types, turn to page 101.

Guidance

The design of the datafile structure, including the way it is displayed on screen, varies considerably from program to program.

could use a spreadsheet program, or even one of the more powerful word-processing programs. These applications will let you input and sort the type of information kept on the filing cards. However, a database program will also allow you to generate more complicated searches and reports. In addition, Gurdip realises that once people start using the database they may then think of other things to do with it that a spreadsheet or word-processing program would be unable to do.

3. Designing the datafile

In a database, a 'datafile' is the word used for a collection of records. (Often, the word database is used.) The file Gurdip requires is fairly simple – there will be one record for each member of staff. However, each piece of information which needs to be accessed in its own right requires a field. (For example, users who want to find a person's address will start by searching for the person's surname, so the surname needs a field to itself. Separating the names into Surname and First Name will also make it possible to sort properly.) Ideally, a database record structure should have separate fields for the various components of the address (e.g. street, town, county, postcode, etc.).

Before she sets up the database form on screen, Gurdip looks at the source information and breaks down the information into discrete fields, accompanied by the names of each field she requires and their length (i.e. how many characters they will need).

When you set up a database, the program may ask you for the type of data to be entered. Before setting up your database you should look at the source data, think about how people will want to use the database and jot down the appropriate field names, lengths and types.

4. Entering the database and naming the file

The database program which all the staff use is shown on Gurdip's computer screen as an icon.

You may not be presented with icons to choose from – in this case you may be presented with a menu option or you might even have to key in commands to start up the program.

When the program asks her to select a file, Gurdip selects NEW to create a new datafile. Your program may not automatically ask you to select a file, in which case you may need to select NEW or CREATE NEW FILE from a FILE menu. You might be asked to name your document before you enter the text. Remember that the name you give your file should reflect its purpose and perhaps the version number. (Gurdip uses STAFF1.)

5. The length of fields

When Gurdip creates a field for a piece of information, she has to allocate a name to it. The field name must not be confused with its content. For example, the field called Surname will contain different surnames (e.g. Fraser-Hardy).

The length of each field is determined by the length of the longest piece of data that is going to be put in that field. Therefore, if you look at the filing cards you can see that Fraser-Hardy is the longest surname, containing 12 characters. However, as it is likely that other sales staff will join, Gurdip allows for longer surnames and sets the field length at 16 characters. When you set up your fields do remember to take into account what people may need to enter into them in the future. On the other hand, unnecessarily large fields can waste space, slow things down and be a nuisance when it comes to printing reports from the database.

Insert Field

Type a width that will best fit your entries. Type a new height if you want a multi-line field.

Name: Surname
Width: 16
Height: 1

OK
Cancel
Help

Guidance

When you set up your fields do remember to take into account what may need to be added in the future. Remember also that unnecessarily large fields can waste space, slow things down and be a nuisance when it comes to printing reports from the database. Codes should be used where appropriate.

Field	Length
Title	4
Surname	16
First Name	10
Address1	18
Address2	15
Post Code	8
Telephone	12
Date of Birth	8
Shop	1

Gurdip's table, showing the fields she wants and their length

6. Specifying field types

When setting up the fields Gurdip's program does not require her to specify the type of data for each field. In this case all the fields, except for the date, are text fields.

The information will be displayed as text unless formatted otherwise. Therefore Gurdip sets her cursor in the Date of Birth field, pulls down the format menu and selects Number and then Date format.

Guidance

Text fields are sometimes known as alphanumeric fields because they can contain both characters and numbers.

You may need to specify a field as numeric if you want to sort entries in numerical order or if you wish to undertake calculations. Your database may allow you to specify more specialised field types, such as date, time and pound sterling (£).

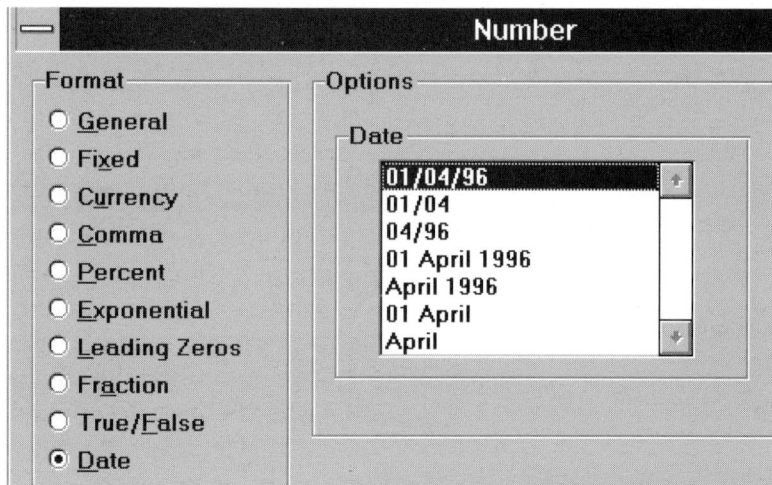

Number

Format
○ General
○ Fixed
○ Currency
○ Comma
○ Percent
○ Exponential
○ Leading Zeros
○ Fraction
○ True/False
⦿ Date

Options

Date
01/04/96
01/04
04/96
01 April 1996
April 1996
01 April
April

Note that Gurdip keeps the Telephone field as a text field. This is because it is not going to be formatted as a number. It will not be sorted numerically nor justified right.

Gurdip uses a single character field for the shops, as there are only five shops, and she only needs to enter the first character, e.g. D for Dover, F for Folkestone, A for Ashford, C for Canterbury, M for Maidstone.

This is how Gurdip's database screen looks once she has finished setting up all the fields:

```
         Title: [__]  First Name: [_____]  Surname: [_____]
      Address1: [_____]
      Address2: [_____]
          Town: [_____]
     Post Code: [_____]
     Telephone: [_____]
 Date of Birth: [_____]
          Shop: [_]
```

7. Entering the data

All the staff details have been written down on the filing cards shown on page 30. Gurdip needs to enter this information into the datafile. She takes the first record card.

In this instance, all the data needs to be entered, in accordance with the way the database has been designed.

Gurdip selects the DATA ENTRY facility from her screen. Your program may require you to ADD DATA, or a blank record may automatically appear when you enter the file.

Gurdip's cursor appears in the first blank field, 'Surname'. She enters the data from the record card according to the sequence of specified fields: note the 'Shop' field. In this field Gurdip keys in a single character code – D for Dover, F for Folkestone, etc.

The record cards above show the details that Gurdip has to enter in order to update the file. When you enter them into your own file, remember that:

● the Surname is to be entered before the First Name
● the dates of birth should be entered in a consistent format, in this case DD/MM/YY
● when there is no data specified (e.g. no second line of address), leave the field blank

Note that the data is deployed record by record. In Gurdip's program this is called FORM VIEW.

```
MARK HARTSHORN, MR        DOVER
21 CHESTNUT CLOSE
BUCKLAND
DOVER DO7 8YU
01304 45345
DATE OF BIRTH      23/03/66
```

```
         Title: [Mr]  First Name: [Mark]  Surname: [Hartshorn]
      Address1: [21 Chestnut Close]
      Address2: [Buckland]
          Town: [Dover]
     Post Code: [DO7 8YU]
     Telephone: [01304 45345]
 Date of Birth: [23/03/66]
          Shop: [D]
```

This is how Gurdip's data appears

8. Checking the details against the record cards to ensure accuracy

After entering the new details, Gurdip checks her input for mistakes. She looks through the whole file by using the PAGE UP and PAGE DOWN keys to move between them. If you have a program that uses a mouse, you may be able to use the mouse to move between records. Gurdip found that she had made several mistakes. She had put some of the names in the wrong way round, and had sometimes put the town names in the 'Address2' field.

If you find that you have made a mistake, put your cursor in the field containing the mistake and correct it. You may need to delete the incorrect data first by using one of the delete functions, or you may be able to overtype.

9. Displaying the data

The information in the database can be displayed on the screen as required. In this case Gurdip merely wants to check that all the data has been entered, and entered correctly. However, displaying each record in FORM VIEW, that is one by one, is not the most efficient way of looking at the information. Gurdip selects the LIST option from the VIEW menu, which displays all the records in a table format. Most database programs will allow you to do this and some even do it automatically.

You may prefer this because it allows you to see a summarised version of the whole file from which you can pick the record you want to view or print.

See if you can display your file in a table format. Gurdip does this by using the LIST command, which is found within the VIEW options.

	Surname	First Name	Title	Address1	Address2	Town	Post Code	Tele
1	Hartshorn	Mark	Mr	21 Chestnut Close	Buckland	Dover	DO7 8YU	01304
2	Argyle	Judith	Mrs	99 Barley Close		Dover	DO7 1JU	01304
3	Kaushal	Sukhinder	Miss	43 Hall Farm Road	Sandgate	Folkestone	FO3 4RT	0130:
4	Hucker	David	Mr	2 Avenue Road	Hales Place	Canterbury	CA5 6TT	01227
5	Squires	Shirley	Miss	4 Richmond Drive	Sevington	Ashford	AS5 6GF	0123:
6	Fraser-Hardy	Rosemary	Miss	10 Chapel Street		Canterbury	KF5 3WE	01227
7	Lysencko	Keith	Mr	57 Park Road	Hales Place	Canterbury	CA5 6TT	01227
8	Andrews	Linford	Mrs	1 Mortimer Drive	Buckland	Dover	WM13 6BH	01304
9	Robinson	Jef	Mr	7 Campion Rd	Cheriton	Folkestone	NA19 6GH	0130:
10	Delaney	Clare	Ms	7 Campion Rd	Cheriton	Folkestone	NA19 6GH	0130:
11	Dawe	Harry	Mr	49 Chestnut Close	Hinxhill	Maidstone	MA6 3TR	0162:
12	Hinds	Catherine	Miss	110 Dover Road		Maidstone	MA16 7SR	0162:
13								

10. Sorting the data

The new data that Gurdip has added to the file will be displayed in the order in which it was entered. To see it in alphabetical order of surnames, it will require an alphabetic sort. Sorting is the process by which data is put into a required order. In order to display it this way, Gurdip selects the SORT option from the TOOLS menu and then selects an alphabetic sort.

When you are sorting records in your database, remember to take into account that there may be more than one entry with the same surname, so make sure that you specify First Name as the second sort field.

11. Searching

Gurdip wants to test the search facilities and decides to search for all staff who live in the Folkestone area.

Guidance

This is a good example of using appropriate software to display information, thus meeting the performance criteria 3.2 at LEVELS 2 and 3.

To do this, she chooses the QUERY option and specifies that she only wants to look at those records for the staff who work in the Folkestone shop. She therefore opens up the new query option and enters the following information:

```
┌─────────────────────────────────────────────────────────────────┐
│ ─                          New Query                              │
│                                                                   │
│  Please give this query a name:     Folkestone Shop               │
│  Create query sentences below, and then choose Apply Now to see all records that match the criteria. │
│                                                                   │
│   Choose a field to compare:     How to compare the field:    Value to compare the field to: │
│  A. │Shop          │↧│  B. │is equal to    │↧│  E. │F           │ │
│                              ○ And                                │
│                              ○ Or                                 │
│  F. │              │↧│  G. │               │↧│  L. │            │ │
└─────────────────────────────────────────────────────────────────┘
```

You will notice from the above that it is possible to enter MULTIPLE CRITERIA and even MULTIPLE CONDITIONS required against the specified fields (i.e. 'F' in the Town field and 'Peter' in the First Name field.

After entering the new details, Gurdip checks her input for mistakes. She looks through the whole file by using the PAGE UP and PAGE DOWN keys to move between them. If you have a program that uses a mouse, you may be able to use the mouse. Gurdip found that she had made several mistakes. She had put some of the names in the wrong way round, and had sometimes put the town names in the 'Address2' field.

? **HELP**
There are many ways of setting up searches. It is common to base the search on more than one criterion. It is suggested that you explore the facilities available in your program. These skills are particularly valuable when exploring large databases, for example some of those available on CD-ROM and the Internet. If you need help with search logic, turn to page 99.

If you find that you have made a mistake, put your cursor in the field with the mistake and correct it. You may need to delete the incorrect data first by using one of the delete functions, or you may be able to overtype.

12. Printing the information

The names and addresses from the database file are not automatically displayed on the screen, but Gurdip can preview all the information by choosing the PREVIEW option from the PRINT menu.

Guidance

For help on backing up see page 66 and also Assignment 13, page 95.

13. Saving and backing up the file

Many database programs save the data automatically upon leaving the program. Gurdip needs to make sure that the file is saved so she saves it using the name STAFF1. Just in case of accidents, make a back up copy by saving the file again, either on a floppy disk or in another directory.

Guidance

In *Windows*-based programs you can shut down by double-clicking the mouse pointer in the top left-hand corner of the relevant window.

14. Closing down

Gurdip shuts down the database program by using the EXIT option from the FILE menu.

Ensure that you shut down the program in the correct sequence, making certain the data is intact.

EVIDENCE
Assignment 7 provides an opportunity to produce evidence of achievement in setting up and using a simple database.

6   Keeping a record of sales

The shop manager of the Dover branch, Judith Argyle, is keeping a close watch on the sales. She maintains a chart in the back room of the shop, which shows how much money is coming in every week. The income is divided into two categories, Cash and Credit. Here are the returns shown on the sales chart.

Week1	5917.60	789.59
Week2	6736.86	341.95
Week3	4500.83	232.19
Week4	4003.68	843.49
Week5	2579.76	448.84
Week6	4404.04	927.83
Week7	2837.73	493.72
Week8	8462.16	1129.10
Week9	9633.70	488.98
Week10	6436.32	332.02
Week11	4844	1020.61
Week12	3121.50	543.09
Week13	9308.37	1242.01
TOTAL	72787.09	8833.42

Judith has decided that this sort of record keeping would be best handled by a spreadsheet (an application that uses columns and rows to store and manipulate data, and also makes calculations). Keeping the information on a spreadsheet system would provide much greater flexibility and from this it would be possible to generate different types of graph to display differences and trends. Judith knows that doing all this by hand would be tedious.

The IT skills Judith will use include:

▶ setting up the spreadsheet structure;
▶ entering the data;
▶ saving the spreadsheet;
▶ printing it out;
▶ appraising its effectiveness.

You can practise these skills by following the steps that Judith takes and carrying out the equivalent processes on your own computer.

Practise

1. Opening up the spreadsheet

Judith chooses the spreadsheet application from the main menu and is presented with a blank spreadsheet on screen.

B3					
	A	B	C	D	E
1					
2					
3					
4					
5					
6					
7					
8					
9					
10					
11					
12					
13					
14					
15					

When you get into your spreadsheet, you will notice that the screen is divided into columns labelled with letters, and rows labelled with numbers. The position at which each column and row cross each other is known as a 'cell'. Each cell is identified by its column letter and row number and is given a cell reference (e.g. the cell that is in column B and in row 3 will have a reference of B3). When you place the cursor in a cell, its reference will be displayed on screen. Try moving the cursor around the screen and watch the cell reference change accordingly.

2. Entering the spreadsheet row headings

Guidance

Each cell may contain text (as labels), numerical data, or formulas (which perform calculations upon numerical data). As you key in data, it appears on a data entry line at the top of the screen. Sometimes the data appears in the cell itself too. When you have entered the data into the cell, it disappears from the data entry line.

With the blank spreadsheet on screen, Judith positions the cursor in the top left-hand corner. She enters the following headings along row 1:

WEEKS   CASH   CREDIT   TOTAL

When she keyed in 'WEEKS', Judith used the right arrow key to get to the next cell, and 'WEEKS' was entered as a heading. Her cursor moved automatically to the next cell, which in this case was **B1**.

When you key in your headings, make sure you are in the top left-hand cell. The reference should be A1. Type in the word WEEKS and enter it using the Enter key or the right arrow key.

You should now be in cell B1. (Use the cursor keys to move to B1 if you are not already there.) Now enter the rest of the column headings. These are known as labels. (Labels are text descriptions, usually shown at the top of columns and the beginning of rows.)

3. Entering the income for each week

Judith enters the data shown on the previous page into her spreadsheet, under the appropriate column headings:

When entering the information she made several decisions, namely:

- She inserted an empty row after the first row. This was to make the column headings stand out more.
- She inserted Wk in front of each week number. This was to make the spreadsheet process the week numbers as text labels.
- She put in a TOTALS label at the bottom, leaving an empty line between week 13 and the Totals row. This was because she knew she would want to calculate some totals.

	A	B	C	D
1	WEEKS	CASH	CREDIT	TOTAL
2				
3	Week 1	5917.6	789.59	
4	Week 2	6736.86	341.95	
5	Week 3	4500.93	232.19	
6	Week 4	4003.68	843.49	
7	Week 5	2579.76	448.84	
8	Week 6	4404.04	927.83	
9	Week 7	2837.73	493.72	
10	Week 8	8462.16	1129.1	
11	Week 9	9633.7	488.98	
12	Week 10	6436.32	332.02	
13	Week 11	4844.44	1020.61	
14	Week 12	3121.5	543.09	
15	Week 13	9308.37	1242.01	
16				
17	TOTALS			
18				
19				

When you key in data, enter it as shown above. Also check over your data carefully to avoid any mistakes. Don't worry if the data you enter appears to be truncated. The information is all still there and will appear when you change format (see 5, below).

4. Saving the spreadsheet and the source data

Having entered the data it is good practice to save your work. Judith saves her spreadsheet using the save option, which is on the FILE menu (you may find it on a different menu). When prompted, she gives it a name – SALES1. When you save your spreadsheet, give it a name that reflects its purpose so that you can retrieve it easily in the future. Judith also files the original, handwritten data. This is particularly important with spreadsheets, in case there is any question of accuracy.

5. Changing the formats

Numbers can appear in different ways, but the format of the spreadsheet needs to be tailored to suit one's needs. When Judith entered the data, it did not appear with the symbols of pounds and pence. The credit entry for week 8 appeared as 1129.1 (see cell C10 in the diagram above) and the cash for week 9 appeared as 9633.7. This can appear a little confusing. It is good practice to display pounds and pence by showing both as decimal figures, with two decimal places.

Before				After		
Week 8	8462.16	1129.1		Week 8	8462.16	1129.10

Judith does this by highlighting the cells she wishes to change into decimal format, then selecting the FORMAT menu and selecting Number and then 2 Fixed decimals.

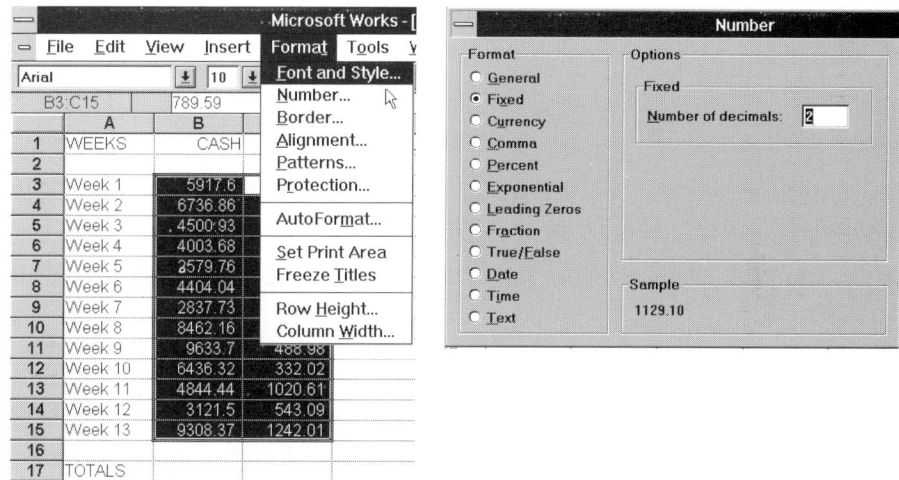

You may find a different way of doing this. Spreadsheets will normally allow you to select a currency format – the disadvantage of this is that it prefixes all numbers with the pound (£) sign.

In spreadsheets labels generally contain text, and text is customarily displayed aligned to the left. If you look at the screen display above, you will see that, in this case, the first column, that containing the week number, is displayed against the left-hand side of the cell (in other words it is aligned left). If Judith had not entered Week before the actual week number, the spreadsheet would have treated the data as a number to be processed and would have aligned it to the right.

All the columns can be reduced in width. This can be done by highlighting them, as one block, and then selecting the column width facility and amending as desired.

Sometimes labels exceed this length. They will appear truncated. One solution is to abbreviate the label sensibly. Another is to alter the column width. This is especially common with the first column. On *Windows* spreadsheets this can done by dragging the column divider grid lines from side to side with the mouse. Alternatively, you can put your cursor in column A and mark (or select) the whole column. Then, from the menu, select the Format and then Column width. You should now be able to specify the width.

Guidance

All numbers can be lined up against the left side of the column by highlighting the appropriate cells and using the appropriate icon or formatting command.

Guidance

Spreadsheets normally have a standard column width of ten characters, which can be narrowed and widened.

Guidance

Some packages also offer automatic 'best fit' to data contained in cells.

? HELP
If you need more help with formulas and functions, turn to page 113.

Guidance

The advantage of using the SUM function is that if a row or column is inserted or deleted, the SUM formula will automatically be adjusted to take the alteration into account.

? HELP
Note that some spreadsheet programs allow you to replicate by clicking on the COPY and PASTE icons.

6. Entering formulas

Judith's next step is to enter an appropriate formula into the spreadsheet so that it will automatically calculate the running totals for the amounts spent on items. Using such formulas ensures that the spreadsheet calculations can be automatically updated as numerical data are changed. Judith moves the cursor to the cell D3, which is under the heading 'TOTAL', and keys in a formula that will add up the income in row 3 for week 1. In this case she needs to add up the numbers from cell B3 to C3. The simplest method, in this case, is to enter the formula =B3+C3. The equals sign tells the computer that the next entry is for a formula, otherwise it will be treated as text. Judith decides to use what is called the SUM function. Instead of telling the spreadsheet to perform the calculation 'B3+C3', Judith asks it to perform 'SUM(B3:C3)'. Hence the entry that Judith keys into cell D3 is '=SUM(B3:C3)'

You will find that the symbols used for formulas vary from spreadsheet to spreadsheet, so the start of your formula may need to be a '+' or '@'. Find out from your manual or on-screen help what your program uses.

7. Replicating a formula

To add up the spending in all the other rows, Judith needs to enter the same formula in the remaining cells in column D (although the row numbers in the cell references will change). She could enter them separately in each cell, but this would be time-consuming. When you need to repeat a formula in a lot of cells it is best to use the replicating facilities available on your spreadsheet. Judith replicates the formula to the other cells in column D by highlighting the cell to be copied (D3), extending the highlight down to include the cells she wants to fill (D4 to D15) and then choosing the FILL DOWN option from the EDIT menu. Using this she replicates (copies) the contents of the selected cell down to the remaining cells – D4 to D15 – in column D.

This form of copying is called 'replication'. Replication is a specific form of copying, commonly associated with spreadsheets, which ensures that the relative values are replicated (i.e. it automatically changes the cell references in the formula). Look at the formulas below and see how all the cell references have been changed.

D
TOTAL
=SUM(B3:C3)
=SUM(B4:C4)
=SUM(B5:C5)
=SUM(B6:C6)
=SUM(B7:C7)
=SUM(B8:C8)
=SUM(B9:C9)
=SUM(B10:C10)
=SUM(B11:C11)
=SUM(B12:C12)
=SUM(B13:C13)
=SUM(B14:C14)
=SUM(B15:C15)

8. Generating totals for the cash and credit

A total is needed at the bottom of cash and credit columns (in the 'Total' row, starting in cell A17). Judith does this by entering the formula '=SUM(B3:B15)' into cell B17. She then copies (replicates) this formula into cells C17 and D17.

The spreadsheet calculates the total and the figure 816250.51 appears in cell D17.

The total income should be 81620.51. Judith has already calculated this by manually adding up the data.

	A	B	C	D	E	F
1	WEEKS	CASH	CREDIT	TOTAL		
2						
3	Week 1	5917.6	789.59			
4	Week 2	6736.86	341.95			
5	Week 3	4500.93	232.19			
6	Week 4	4003.68	843.49			
7	Week 5	2579.76	448.84			
8	Week 6	4404.04	927.83			
9	Week 7	2837.73	493.72			
10	Week 8	8462.16	1129.1			
11	Week 9	9633.7	488.98			
12	Week 10	6436.32	332.02			
13	Week 11	4844.44	1020.61			
14	Week 12	3121.5	543.09			
15	Week 13	9308.37	1242.01			
16						
17	TOTALS					

If your total is different, carefully check all the entries in all the columns. Compare your data with the source data. If all the figures appear to be correct, then check your formulas.

9. Saving the spreadsheet

HELP
If you need help with naming files, turn to page 107.

Judith saves her spreadsheet using the SAVE option which she finds on the FILE menu (you may find it elsewhere). When prompted she gives it a new name – 'SALES2'. She does this as a safety precaution because, for the moment, she wants to keep the original file with the original data. When you save your spreadsheet it is important that you give it a name that reflects its purpose, so that you can retrieve it easily in the future.

10. Printing the spreadsheet

Judith prints out her spreadsheet using the PRINT option from the FILE menu. This is what it looks like.

Prior to printing, check whether the printer is 'on-line' and has paper in it. Find the print options on the program you are using. Gridlines and cell references are usually available as options. Print out your spreadsheet – it should look like Judith's.

11. Reviewing the effectiveness of the spreadsheet

Once Judith has finished the spreadsheet, she shows it to Clare Delaney, the Dover branch Assistant Manager. They agree it could be improved by:

● setting up columns for other items of income, expenditure and VAT;
● presenting the data in a graphical format, such as a bar chart, to make it easier to understand. (The next activity gives some suggestions for this.)
● adding data and giving a title to the spreadsheet;
● generating a weekly average return.

Also, the daily takings still have to be added up as weekly totals before the income data can be entered into the spreadsheet. Ideally, this too would be computerised.

Can you think of any more improvements that could be made?

EVIDENCE

Assignment 10 provides an opportunity to produce evidence of achievement in setting up a spreadsheet and reviewing its effectiveness.

7   Preparing sales graphs from spreadsheets

The shop manager, Judith Argyle, wants to report the sales figures to her staff, and to Eileen MacQuarry, the Managing Director. Previously, she has presented this information in the form of hand-drawn bar graphs. However, now that the information is stored on a spreadsheet, she feels that it could be presented more clearly and efficiently using the graphic facilities which her spreadsheet program offers.

For her next presentation, Judith wants to prepare suitable graphs to show the actual income to date.

The IT skills she will use to do this include:

▶ creating graphs from spreadsheet data;
▶ assessing different graph formats on screen to find the most suitable one for the purpose;
▶ printing graphs;
▶ saving graphs.

You can practise these skills by following the steps that Judith takes and carrying out the equivalent processes on your own computer (providing it has the facility to create graphs).

Practise

Guidance

You could use a dedicated graphics package to create graphs. It could offer you more power, but you may be required to enter data directly.

1. Selecting the spreadsheet data

Judith has already created a spreadsheet file with all the data she wants to use in the graphs ('SALES2' – in the previous activity). She opens this file to bring it up on her screen. Look at page 38 to remind yourself of the layout.

The data that Judith wants to convert into a graph are:

● the text labels for the columns (in column A);
● the cash sales (in column B);
● the credit sales so far (in column C).

Judith's software allows her to select columns that are adjacent to each other, so she selects columns A, B, and C which are displayed side by side. If you are working in a program that allows you to select specific columns, you will need to specify the range of cells you want converted to a graph within that program's GRAPH facility.

Judith highlights weeks 1 to 13 in columns A, B and C and then selects the COPY icon from the toolbar. You may have to key in the specific range of cells you want to copy, or highlight the selection cell by cell. If there is no COPY icon on your screen, you will need to use an EDIT menu or a COPY menu.

The figure on the next page shows the block of cells that Judith copied and has selected for displaying as a graph. They include the WEEKS column for the x-series labels, the CASH SALES column, and the CREDIT column. The top row of the block is also shaded. This text will be used as legends explaining the purpose of the columns in the bar graph.

	A	B	C
1	WEEKS	CASH	CREDIT
2			
3	Week 1	5917.60	789.59
4	Week 2	6736.86	341.95
5	Week 3	4500.93	232.19
6	Week 4	4003.68	843.49
7	Week 5	2579.76	448.84
8	Week 6	4404.04	927.83
9	Week 7	2837.73	493.72
10	Week 8	8462.16	1129.10
11	Week 9	9633.70	488.98
12	Week 10	6436.32	332.02
13	Week 11	4844.44	1020.61
14	Week 12	3121.50	543.09
15	Week 13	9308.37	1242.01

Highlight the cells on your sheet in the same way or, if necessary, specify the range of cells you want to represent in the graph.

2. Selecting the chart option

To create a graph, Judith selects the NEW CHART icon from her toolbar.

The program then asks her what kind of graph she would like. She selects the default, which is a bar graph.

A NEW CHART icon on a *Windows* toolbar

This is what her program produces.

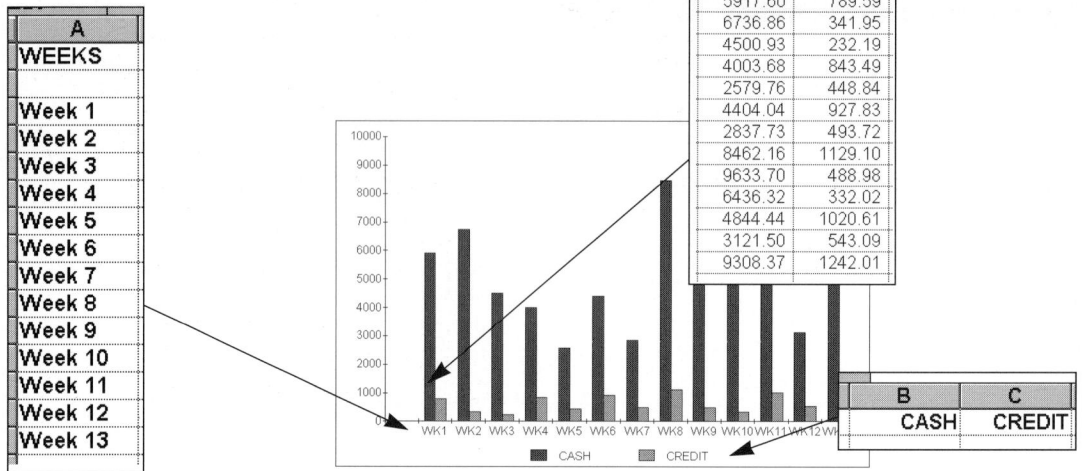

	B	C
	CASH	**CREDIT**
	5917.60	789.59
	6736.86	341.95
	4500.93	232.19
	4003.68	843.49
	2579.76	448.84
	4404.04	927.83
	2837.73	493.72
	8462.16	1129.10
	9633.70	488.98
	6436.32	332.02
	4844.44	1020.61
	3121.50	543.09
	9308.37	1242.01

The program has taken the first column of the spreadsheet (WEEKS) and displayed this along the bottom so that the weeks form the horizontal axis for the graph, in other words the X-series. The second and third columns of the selected data are graphed as the Y-series (the vertical bars). Because Judith has highlighted the text labels at the top of the spreadsheet column, they have been converted into the legend (CASH and CREDIT) which shows what the bars represent.

HELP
If you need help in understanding X-series labels, turn to page 113.

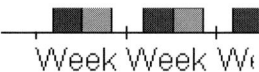

3. Modifying the spreadsheet labels

Note that the labels for the weeks have been truncated – some of the information is missing.

In this case, these are the first four characters in the spreadsheet column A (for weeks 1–13). Judith decides that the best thing to do is to edit the data in the spreadsheet. She uses the search and replace option, replacing Week with Wk, and then views the chart again.

4. Stacked bars

Judith wants to stack cash and credit on top of one another, showing the overall sales returns as well as the components. Her program allows her to select the STACKED BARS, and view them in 3-D (three dimensions).

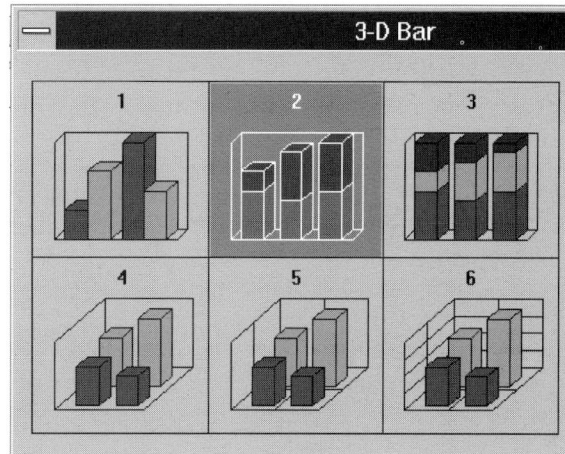

Your program may create graphs in a different way. Find its graph facility and specify the type of graph you want it to create.

5. Entering titles

To make the graph look more complete, Judith adds titles to it, using the EDIT menu. She enters the main title 'Sales for the First Quarter', and then she enters 'WEEKS' for the X-axis and 'POUNDS' for the Y-axis.

You may find a TITLE option in an INSERT menu or a GRAPH menu.

Judith's program allows her to alter the font sizes from the toolbar. She highlights the main title and changes the font size to 14.

Your program may let you do these things in other ways.

This is what Judith's completed 3D bar graph looks like.

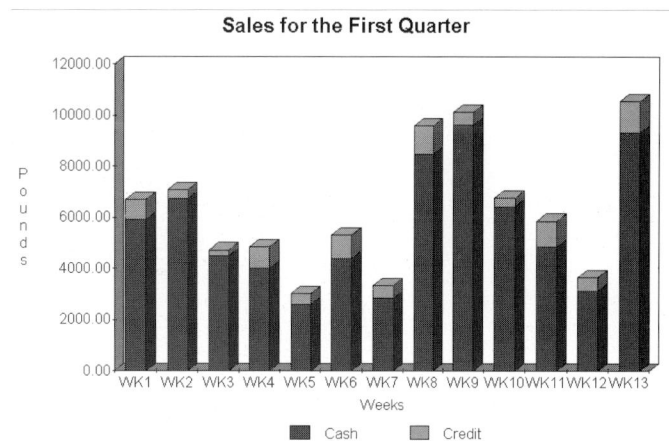

6. Naming the graph

As Judith is worried about finding this work again, she decides to give it a unique name. The program she uses automatically allocates a name to every graph, giving them names such as Chart1, Chart2, etc. Judith decides to RENAME the graph '3D-BAR'. This name will also make it easier for her to identify that file as containing a bar graph when she wants to retrieve it. On her program whenever a spreadsheet is saved, the associated graphs are also saved and can be called up again.

Your program may not do this so you will need to check whether the graphs are automatically saved.

7. Changing the presentation

Judith decides that she is not very sure about the presentation and would like to explore different ways of presenting the same data using a line graph. She returns to the toolbar and selects the LINE GRAPH icon:

Many programs offer a choice of line graphs

Your program may show the types of graph that are available in a different way. Some programs have a pull-down menu called GALLERY; on others GRAPHS is an option within the FORMAT menu.

Judith's program offers her a number of presentations.

After Judith has made her choice, the program produces the following graph.

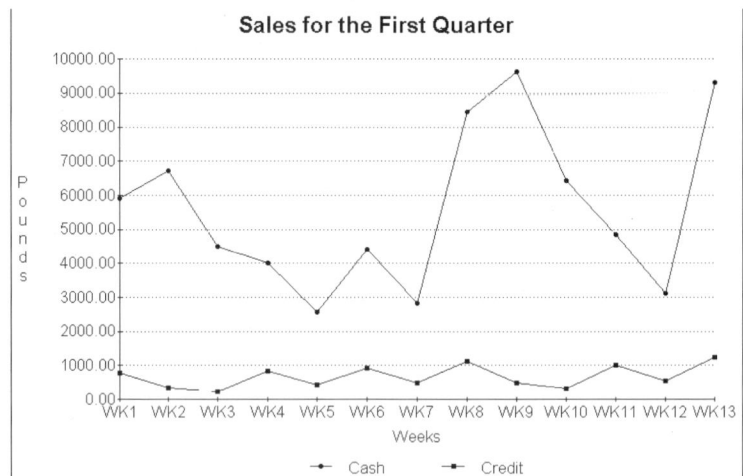

You may be able to vary the style of presentation on the package you are using. Try a few styles and choose the clearest.

8. Printing the graphs and shut down

After saving the final versions of her graphs, Judith prints them out, saves the spreadsheet with the additional graphs as SALES2 and exits from the spreadsheet application and the system.

9. Appraising the graphs

Do you think Judith would have saved time and presented the information in a better way if she had drawn the graphs by hand, using coloured pencils?

How might she have used a pie chart?

Which graphs were most effective?

How could a moving weekly average be shown best?

When you have printed out your graphs, show them to your tutor and fellow students and ask them how effective they think the graphs are in presenting the selected information.

EVIDENCE
Assignment 5 provides an opportunity to produce evidence of achievement in creating business graphs.

8   Working safely

Most people do not think about the potential hazards of working with computers. However, health and safety at work are very important considerations – and using computers can be dangerous!

A few years ago computers were hardly used at all in the Remedy shops. When the first computer was introduced, this was done in a fairly haphazard manner and nobody was fully aware of the health and safety issues that might arise.

There are physical hazards associated with working with computers. For example, poorly adjusted seating or poor visibility can, over a period of time, result in damage to health. Working with computers can be very intensive, therefore it is often stressful and likely to cause fatigue. If such fatigue can be minimised, the good health of workers can be maintained and it is even probable that productivity will be enhanced.

Specific legislation, administered by the Health & Safety Executive, applies to the use of computer equipment including keyboard, desk, chair and screen. Failure to comply with this legislation can result in hefty fines.

As a result of these considerations, Eileen MacQuarry, the owner and Managing Director of Remedy, is acutely conscious of the need to make all the staff who use computers at the Remedy shops aware of their potential dangers. Although she is constantly involved in reorganising and updating the working environment in all the shops, it is not always easy to get others to take notice of health and safety issues.

Eileen has drawn a diagram which shows the hazards present in one of the shops before it was reorganised and has made it compulsory for all users of the computer system to complete a 'spot the hazards' exercise as part of their induction to using the computer system. She has asked Clare Delaney, from the Dover branch, to undertake the exercise. The diagram is shown below.

During this exercise Clare will:

● report back to Eileen MacQuarry on the hazards she finds;
● take note of any other hazards not yet identified.

Look at the picture above and spot as many IT-related hazards as Clare can.

Make yourself aware of health and safety by following the steps below.

Practise

1. Identifying potential hazards

Study the diagram that Eileen has prepared and see how many hazards you can spot. Circle each one.

Compare your results with the list below

cables	These should not be trailing all over the floor. Tripping over them can result in injury and damage to equipment. Multiple plugs and extension leads should be avoided. Work stations should be sited close to the power points. If this is not possible, cables should be laid under tape or bridged to the equipment.
positioning of screen	Correct positioning of the screen is crucial to avoid muscle strain in the neck and shoulders. All screens must be adjustable to suit the user. The screen should be directly in front of you, at a distance that is roughly an arm's length. The top of the the screen (i.e. not the screen casing) should be just above eye level.

positioning of documents	Poor positioning can lead to visual fatigue and muscle tension. Documents should be about the same distance away and the same height as the screen, and near to the screen, in order to minimise re-focusing of the eyes and to minimise the twisting of the neck.
positioning of equipment	Poor positioning can lead to unnecessary strain upon the wrists (keyboard entry) and back (seating position). All chairs must be adjustable – adjust your chair so that your legs fit comfortably under your desk and your forearms are approximately horizontal when using the keyboard. You must keep your back straight and supported. Your feet should rest flat on the floor – if they do not, use a footrest. Shift your position regularly so that you are not sitting in the same position for a long time. Such measures can help prevent repetitive strain injuries (RSI) which are now emerging as one of the hazards particularly associated with working with computers.
glare	This can be caused by reflection from natural light, and artificial lighting that is too bright or in the wrong position. Glare can be minimised by adjusting the background lighting level and/or altering the screen brightness. The use of an anti-glare filter and window blinds can help. Take care, however, to keep anti-glare filters clean, or they will make the screen more difficult to read. The position of the screen is important – it should not be directly facing a window, nor should a window be directly behind it.
lighting	As natural lighting varies it is generally necessary to be able to control it and to be able to supplement it with artificial lighting.
carrying	Take a firm grip when lifting. Do not swivel the back. The back should be straight at the moment the load is taken.
screen flicker	Screen flicker should be avoided. It causes eyestrain. Screen flicker is controlled by the operating frequency of the monitor.
static	Static is the sudden discharge of electricity through a conducting material. Minute electrical charges may accumulate on a metal casing, or on a screen, and this is released by contact with a conducting material, such as the human body. Hence the user may feel a slight shock. This is very unlikely to cause injury. Static can also damage equipment and magnetically stored data. To reduce the risk of static, screens should be cleaned frequently with special anti-static wipes.
heating and ventilation	Rooms need to be well ventilated, especially when there are laser printers and photocopiers, because these emit ozone, a gas that is hazardous. Switch any machines off at night if possible, to minimise the heat generated by electrical equipment.

radiation — VDUs do emit some radiation, but at levels well below the levels considered harmful by such bodies as the National Radiological Protection Board.

2. Reporting back and discussing the hazards

Show your tutor the list of hazards which you identified initially, and note the hazards on Clare's list which you didn't spot. Discuss all of the hazards and identify the particular harm that each one can cause.

Other important issues also need to be considered, such as the effects of IT upon pregnant women and people's eyesight.

Pregnancy

There is little evidence that specifically links working with computers to problems in pregnancy. However, it is good practice to be especially concerned about the working conditions and well-being of pregnant women, whether they are using computers or not.

Eyesight

There is no direct evidence that computer screens damage the eyesight. However, they can aggravate existing defects. Eyes have to be cared for, and working conditions should minimise intensive strain upon the eyes. Do not stare at a screen for too long – focus regularly on something else in the room. Make sure the lighting conditions in the room are adequate and that the monitor is not set up with its back to a window.

3. Consider the way you work with computers

Working with computers can be very intensive and consequently stressful. Think about your working patterns when using a computer. Remember that you should take regular breaks – get up and walk around to loosen your muscles. Make sure your seating is comfortable and provides proper support, particularly for your lower back.

At Head Office, Eileen MacQuarry has decided to undertake regular stress-prevention checks and has introduced the following form.

Checks	Date	Initial	Action taken
Screen Glare			
Radiation			
Wiring			
Heating			
Seating			
Work Surface			

Would a similar form be useful in your own working environment? Discuss the implications with your tutor or supervisor.

Guidance

Further information about the use of computers in the workplace can be obtained from The Royal Society for the Prevention of Accidents (RoSPA)

Cannon House
The Priory
Queensway
Birmingham B4 6BS
Tel: 0121-233 2461

EVIDENCE
Assignment 6 (page 93) provides an opportunity to produce evidence of an understanding of safe working practices.

9 Drawing a plan of the ground floor

Eileen MacQuarry, the Managing Director of Remedy, wants to install a new computer close to the cash tills and the check-out points in all the Remedy shops, but needs to limit access to staff only. She is also aware that the computer must be linked by telephone to the warehouse at Dartford but, as telephone lines are simple to route anywhere, she is not too concerned about this.

Eileen needs to be aware of the appropriate Health and Safety regulations, especially concerning fire and electricity, and also the regulations governing the use of a computer. She has asked Gurdip Bola to draw the floor plan of the Folkestone branch of Remedy on a computer so that it can be readily updated.

The purpose of the plan is to show the complete layout of the shop floor and, within it, the potential location of the computer, shop tills, fire exits, assembly areas in the event of a fire, and telephone points. A hand-drawn plan does exist, but Eileen would like it to be drawn on a computer so that it can be updated easily.

Here is the existing hand-drawn plan, on which the computer drawing will be based.

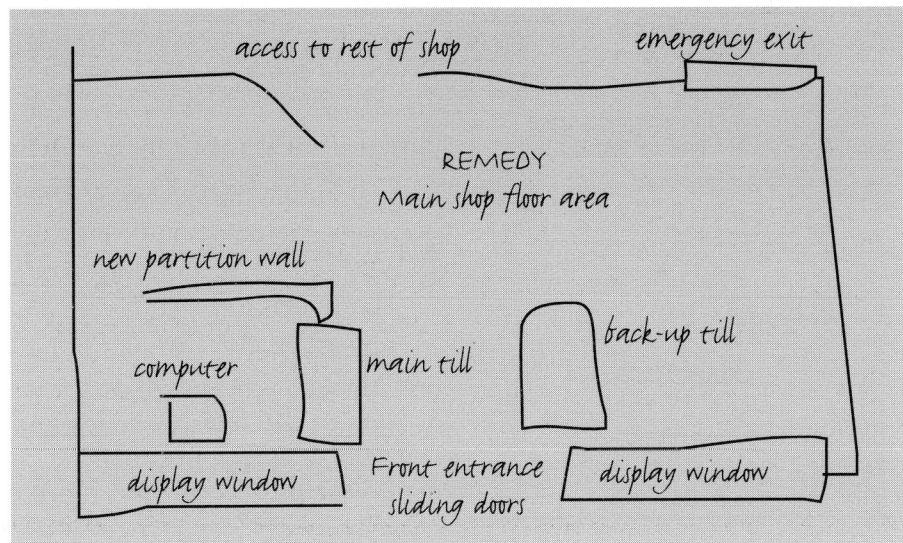

Gurdip has access to a simple drawing program called *Paintbrush*.

The IT skills that Gurdip will use to draw the plan include:

▶ using standard graphics program facilities;

Guidance

Paintbrush is a graphics program which works within the *Windows* environment and is distributed free with *Windows*. In *Windows 95* it is called *Paint*. It is, therefore, used extremely widely. The facilities and icons available in *Paintbrush* are also used in many other graphics programs. The graphics that *Paintbrush* creates can be easily inserted into other *Windows* applications.

This task could be carried out with other graphics programs which have facilities for drawing, shading, and text insertion. You could also use a desktop publishing program, or a computer-aided design (CAD) program which includes tools for drawing, shading, and text and page design. (See pages 104 and 105.)

▶ preparing a line drawing on screen;
▶ shading sections;
▶ inserting text labels;
▶ manipulating shapes.

You can practise these skills by following the steps that Gurdip takes and carrying out the equivalent processes on your own computer.

Practise

1. Entering the graphics program

Paintbrush is shown on Gurdip's screen in the 'Accessories' window. She double-clicks on the *Paintbrush* icon (see below).

Paintbrush

2. Practice on *Paintbrush*

To get used to working with the package, Gurdip practises some simple graphics using the toolbar.

If you are not familiar with this type of program, it is always a good idea to 'doodle' with the drawing facilities before starting on the actual drawing itself.

HELP
If you need help with drawing packages and understanding toolbars, turn to page 104.

Drawing lines
To draw a straight line you need to select the straight line tool by clicking with your mouse on this symbol: ▨. Then move the pointer to the drawing area and click where you want the line to start. Drag the mouse until the line is the right length. Release the button.

If you hold the shift key down when you drag, diagonal lines will be drawn at exactly 45 degrees and vertical lines at exactly 90 degrees.

Guidance

'Drag' means keeping your finger down on the mouse button while you move the mouse.

To draw a curved line, select the curved line tool by clicking on this symbol: ▨. Move the mouse into the drawing area and click and drag until the line is the length you want. Position the pointer above, below, left or right of the line, and click and drag. This will push or pull the line. Drag the pointer until the line curves the way you want it to. Click the mouse again to fix the line.

Guidance

Don't forget to use the on screen help facilities if you are stuck.

Options   Help

When you practise drawing lines, make the screen more colourful by drawing them in different colours and widths – select a line width and a colour before you draw the line (the width choices are shown on the bottom left of the *Paintbrush* screen, and the colour palette runs across the bottom).

Guidance

If you are placing your drawing in another *Windows* application after you have cut or copied it, open the file in the other application, place your cursor where you want the drawing to appear and then paste it in.

The rub-out icon

Cut and paste

If you want to move or copy something you have drawn to another part of your document, the first thing you need to do is to 'cut' round it, using one of the scissors tools: ✂️✂️. One is for regular shapes and the other is for irregular shapes. Select which tool you need, and 'cut' around the area you want to move, copy or cut. To move the shape, click anywhere within the cut-out area and drag it to its new position. If you want to repeat the shape, select the EDIT pull-down menu, select COPY, and then select PASTE (which also appears on the EDIT menu). The cutout appears in the upper left-hand corner of the drawing. Click on it and drag it to where you want it. If you want to delete the shape from your document, simply select CUT from the EDIT menu.

Cleaning up

If you make a mistake while practising, there are several ways to clean it up. The simplest is to choose the rub-out icon and use the pointer as an on-screen eraser. You can change the width of your rub-out by selecting a different line width. If you want to abandon the whole picture and start afresh, select NEW from the FILE menu.

3. Drawing lines and boxes

The outlines of the plan are made up of a number of rectangles. To draw the boundary wall, Gurdip uses a thicker line, which she selects from the screen, and clicks on the unfilled rectangle icon: ▢. She then moves the cursor to a point near the bottom right of the drawing area, then clicks and drags the mouse towards the top right corner, where she releases the mouse button. She then draws the remaining walls. This is what her plan looks like so far.

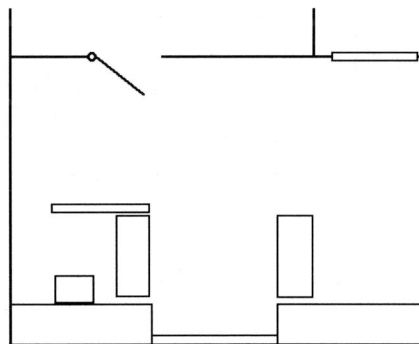

This represents the entire outline of the shop, including the serving area and the tills, and the outline of the side room containing the computer and access to the back room.

Just to be on the safe side, Gurdip saves her plan as a file, using the SAVE AS option from the FILE pull-down menu. She gives her file the name, GFPLAN1.

Guidance

Note that the roller *fills* an area. That means that it will leak through any gaps (i.e. broken lines). It is therefore always a good idea to save the image just before using the roller in case there are any leaks!

4. Shading and colouring

Gurdip decides to use shading to help to distinguish certain areas. She selects a light grey from the colour palette to shade the car-park area, and then selects the roller tool: ⟦icon⟧, which will fill the area with the colour. She applies the colour by clicking the mouse when the tip of the roller is in the car-park area.

Try this yourself by selecting a colour and clicking on the paint roller icon.

To distinguish the partition which shields the planned location of the computer, Gurdip uses the roller tool to apply grey shading. She uses a slighter lighter tone of grey to show the outside area. At this stage, the plan looks like this:

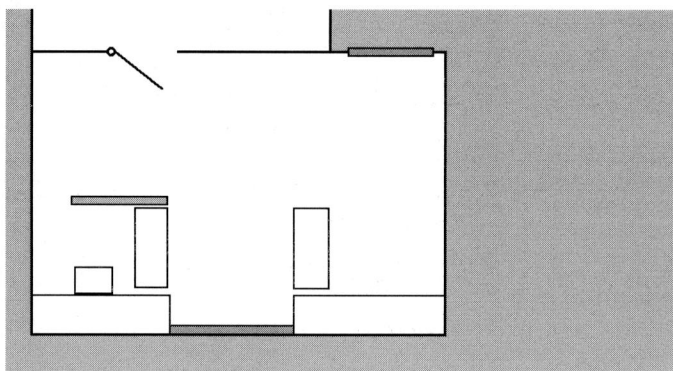

5. Inserting text

Gurdip needs to label the rooms, telephone points, fire exits and the car-park on the plan. To do this she selects the text tool from the toolbar:

abc.

Gurdip chooses attributes for her text (e.g. bold), fonts and typesizes from the TEXT pull-down menu. When she has done this, she clicks where she wants the text to start and keys it in.

When you key in your labels, you do not have to use the same typefaces that Gurdip has used. Try choosing alternatives from the TEXT menu.

HELP
For more information about fonts, see page 103.

6. Finishing touches

Gurdip also identifies electricity power points, using the filled circle icon from the toolbar to create a coloured circle which she then copies and pastes into the relevant areas of the plan, including one as a key (which she labels using the text tool). You could create power points in the same way or you could use the unfilled circle icon and then fill it with another colour using the roller tool.

This is what Gurdip's completed plan looks like.

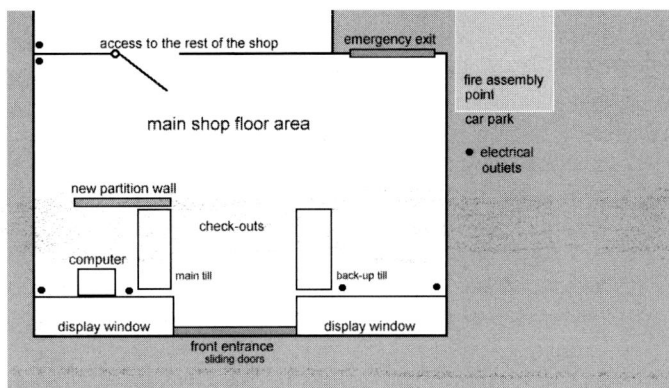

7. Printing

Now Gurdip prints out her plan by choosing PRINT from the FILE pull-down menu, which brings up a box on the screen.

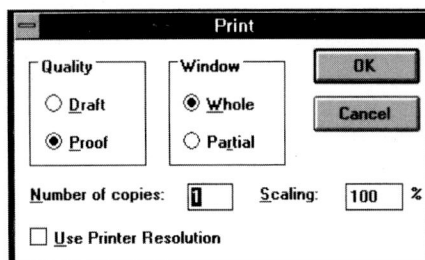

This allows her to specify the number of copies, the quality, etc. Gurdip clicks OK, and the plan is printed out.

8. Saving and exiting from *Paintbrush*

Finally, Gurdip saves her plan as a file using the SAVE AS option from the FILE pull-down menu. She gives her file the name, GFPLAN2.

When you save your plan as a file, you must select the drive you wish to save it on and key in a file name where prompted. Then click on OK.

In order to get out of the program, Gurdip once again uses the FILE pull-down menu. From this she selects EXIT and she is automatically taken out of *Paintbrush*.

9. Comparing methods

The program Gurdip used is relatively simple, but proved adequate for the task. Compare Gurdip's method with other possible ways of creating a plan.

EVIDENCE
Assignment 2 (page 91) provides an opportunity to produce evidence of achievement in using a program to create drawings.

10 Customised letters

Eileen MacQuarry wishes a mailshot to be sent to all staff telling them about the proposed photographic service offered by Photon. She has decided to use the letter that Gurdip prepared (in Activity 4) as a customised letter. Mailshot letters comprise two components. The first is the standard letter text, which is the same for all recipients.

The second component varies from letter to letter – in this case the names and addresses of the sales staff (already stored in the database set up in Activity 5) will be incorporated in the letters.

These two components are then combined to produce a standard letter that will be sent to various addressees. This function is known as 'mail-merge'.

The IT skills Gurdip will use to do this include:

▶ calling up the letter that has already been prepared on computer;
▶ calling up the file of sales staff which has already been prepared on computer;
▶ saving the structure of the standard letter;
▶ running the mailshot.

You can practise these skills by following the steps that Gurdip takes and carrying out the equivalent processes on your own computer.

Practise

Guidance

There are different ways of generating a mail-merge. You can simply use a word-processing program (as long as it has mail-merge facilities). Most database programs have mail-merge facilities, but their text preparation facilities are usually fairly limited. Some databases will allow you to prepare a word-processed letter and then call it up into the database when producing the customised letters.

1. Choosing the application

Gurdip uses an integrated suite of programs from which it is fairly easy to create a mail-merge.

2. Preparation of files

The data for this task already exists in two previously created files. The standard letter is the one created in Activity 4, and the list of sales staff is to be found in the database file created for Activity 5. The data from these two applications can be combined to create a personalised letter.

3. Inserting a data field into the standard letter

Gurdip opens the letter file from Activity 4 (PHOTON1). When she gets into the document, with the cursor at the top of the text for the letter, she selects the INSERT command and then selects DATABASE FIELD. She then chooses the database file created in Activity 5 (STAFF1) and selects the appropriate field names to insert.

When you select the fields you require, make sure you position them in the order that you want them to appear in the letter.

» «First Name» «Surname»
  «Address1»
  «Address2»
  «Town»
  «Post Code»

Dear

An informal quizzing of [...]
development service. Ph[...]
will go a long way to bo[...]
please keep this inform[...]

Insert Field

Fields:
Surname
First Name
Title
Address1
Address2
Town
Post Code
Telephone

Current database:
STAFF1.WDB

Insert
Cancel
Help

Choose Database to
see a list of other
open or recently used
databases.

Database...

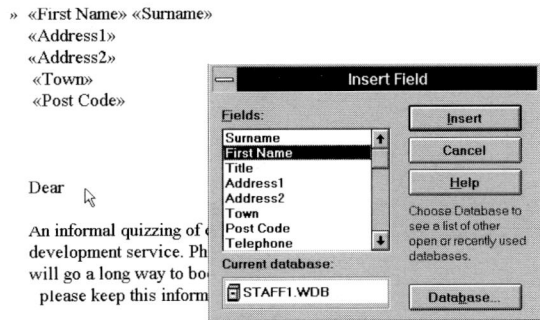

When you have selected a field name, it is automatically inserted on screen. In the figure above, the 'First Name' and 'Surname' field names have been inserted on the first line, separated by a space, the 'Address' field follows on the second line, and 'First Name' has been inserted again, placed after a space following the word 'Dear' in the first line of the letter itself.

You should also include the current date, as appropriate.

4. Printing the letters

Once Gurdip has inserted all the field names she wants, she can run the whole mailshot. The names and addresses from the database file are not automatically displayed on the screen, but Gurdip can preview the letters the mail-merge will create by choosing a PREVIEW option from the PRINT menu. To print the letters she chooses the PRINT MERGE option, and all the letters are printed out with the name and address information in place.

Use your software to create a mailshot, display the letters on screen and print off a sample of the letters.

5. Creating a template

HELP
LEVEL 3 **of IT Core Skills requires
students to set up word-processing
templates. Setting up a mailshot is one way
of doing this. For more information about
style sheets and templates, turn to page 119.**

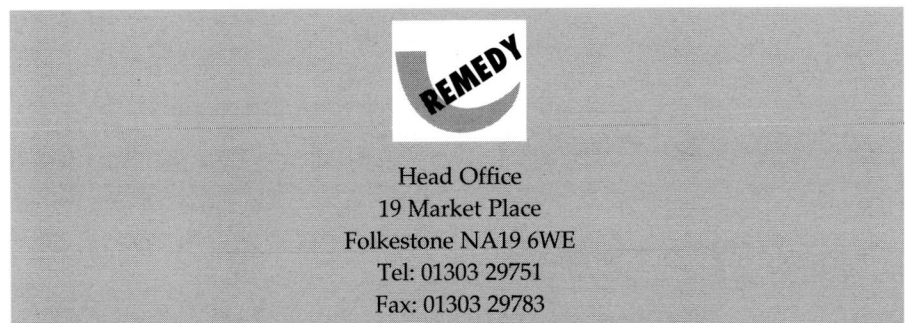

Gurdip realises that there are likely to be many mailshots similar to this one. They will all need the same formatting, including the space for the Remedy logo, and they will need to be linked with the STAFF1 file. She therefore decides to save the structure of the letter as a template. She does this by removing the main body of the text but leaving the merge fields and saving the remaining structure, calling it MAILSHOT.

REMEDY

Head Office
19 Market Place
Folkestone NA19 6WE
Tel: 01303 29751
Fax: 01303 29783

Some, more sophisticated, programs will specifically allow you to save files as templates or style sheets.

Guidance

Labels can also be created by bringing two files together from an existing database file and a new word-processing file. In the word-processing file, use the INSERT menu to select the field names from the appropriate database. When you have inserted all the field names you need, preview them and then print them out.

6. Labels

Labels can be printed on specially prepared label sheets. You will need to adjust the layout to fit the size of the labels you are printing on. A PRINT LABELS option can permit control over:

● the number of labels side by side on a sheet;
● the number of lines per label and the space between labels;
● the page set-up;
● the margins, to suit the paper used.

Guidance

Preparing the printer can be a problem because labels are sticky and the corners can become damaged. Take care not to let them stick and get jammed in the printing equipment. This is one reason why some organisations avoid using labels and, instead, use envelopes which have address windows.

7. Closing down

Gurdip shuts down the files by using the EXIT option from the FILE menu.

11 Evaluation

Guidance

Evaluation is not just something that is done by managers or experts. Even simple uses of IT require some evaluation; for example when deciding whether misleading information, such as a phone number, or a date of birth, should be entered or amended, or whether to refer to somebody else. Millions and millions of pounds have been wasted on IT 'solutions' that have failed. Human beings know how to reason and be critical and these skills need to be applied to IT in order to make the best use of it. You should be able to evaluate your own use of IT where you study and/or at your work placement.

Eileen MacQuarry wants the branch managers to make better use of computer facilities in their shops, particularly as the work involved becomes more complex and time consuming. One way of getting them to do so is to get them to compare and contrast experiences. She has therefore decided to present an informal evaluation to the monthly meeting of the managers on how to improve the use of information technology at the Dover branch of Remedy. The IT skills Eileen will use to do this include:

▶ assessing the ways in which the use of IT affects the efficiency of day-to-day working;
▶ evaluating the improvements that the introduction of IT can make in day-to-day working;
▶ identifying problems associated with integrating IT into the workplace;
▶ identifying ways and means of protecting information from corruption, both accidental and deliberate.

You can practise these skills by following the steps that Eileen takes.

Practise

1. Upgrading the system

Eileen is very appreciative of the way that Remedy staff have tried to make the computer do a variety of tasks but is sure that the system ought now to be upgraded or replaced. She has some strong views about the way the computer is being used.

Eileen is prepared to spend money on equipment but not on extra staff. She is prepared, however, to give the staff extra training but, basically, she wants this to be kept to a minimum as whatever system they employ should be 'user friendly'.

Almost all products seem to be bar-coded nowadays so it makes sense to use a bar code reader at the checkout till in order to log items sold. The bar code reader could form one part of an EPOS system. EPOS stands for **E**lectronic **P**oint **O**f **S**ales and is a system of gathering information regarding sales and stock levels. It is anticipated that a computer will be located near the shop entrance, and will be used at the checkout point. The bar code reader would be linked to the computer and there would be very little need for the person at the till to enter product prices.

Eileen recognises the need to gather further information, and to listen to the views of the staff before proceeding any further but she is already pretty certain that she wants an EPOS system of some sort.

2. Gathering information

The Dover branch of Remedy has only one computer, which is kept in the back room. Eileen decides to sound out the appropriate staff as to how they think their use of information technology could be improved.

You, as the reader, should also ask yourself this question as the practice exercises you have been doing so far are based upon the way the computer is currently being used.

This is a copy of Eileen's notes.

> Judith has kept a manual record of the daily takings. This is added up on the shop till and entered into a spreadsheet periodically in order to generate weekly returns. She recognises that this should be quicker to do on computer, but has not got the necessary bar code equipment nor the POS software which would allow her to do it.
>
> WORD PROCESSING – Judith agrees that word processor is used as a glorified typewriter, mainly to write letters and issue memos – doesn't anticipate using built-in functions like the spelling checker – 'no need to; she spells well'. Anticipates having to design forms using tables or boxes. Hopes to be able to change and move the boxes on the form and feels that she would have to go on a special course to learn to do this.
>
> Staff do not know how to use the range of other facilities. One of the problems is lack of time to learn and explore the other features available.

Guidance

In certain situations, for example if you were less familiar with the current use made of the computer and did not know the users well, you might consider designing a questionnaire to gather information. The sort of questions to ask could include:

- What applications are you using?
- Could you affect, or improve, the efficiency of day-to-day working?
- What further help do you require (e.g. training, equipment)?
- What additional uses do you see for the computer, other than those you use it for now?
- Is the computer system powerful enough?
- How might the computer system be used to do things which are presently done in other ways?
- How might the computer system be used to save time?
- How might the computer system be used to reduce costs?
- How might the computer system be used to increase efficiency?
- How might the computer system be used to improve accuracy?
- Do you think that using the computer system is always the best solution? If not, why?

Judith occasionally needs to print out forms but does not know how to create lines and boxes. Feels the need to go on special course (or, alternatively, to have access to somebody who is highly skilled to give a hand). Does not yet know how to use the other facilities provided; anticipates lack of time in which to learn useful functions and other features.

ROTAS – difficult to computerise.

Another anticipated problem is the fact that the computer will be located in an area immediately adjacent to the main check-out. Even though a new partition wall will be built to screen off the area, noise levels and interruptions are expected to be high. Judith and Clare feel that any further computer purchases should allow for one dedicated to secretarial use.

DATABASE – it is anticipated that the bulk of repetitive hand-written work can be transferred to the computer, particularly stock control and reordering procedures. We need to keep a list of regular customers on the computer. Would like to mail customers with promotions, etc. Database would save time spent looking for the filing cards, and make it easier to find additional information, and add information As it is likely that we will want to use the data for other purposes, it would be better to use a relational database.

An IBM compatible computer, ideally a Pentium or a fast 486, fitted with 16 megabytes of memory and a large hard disk, would be ideal. A fast laser printer would be required to keep pace with the volume of work. A second printer, perhaps a colour inkjet, would be used for presentation purposes. The total costs of such a system need not exceed £2500.

Envelopes and labels – these have been a problem – computerised labels seem to jam the printer.

DATA SECURITY – files should be backed up on to floppy disks. This does not take place, so hard disk getting pretty full. Only a few directories. Recently lost some data. Security password now in place. It has to be keyed in when activating computer. There seem to be no procedures in place for guarding against viruses.

Guidance

A processor is the 'brains' of the computer. Processor chips are described in terms of their power. Personal computers with Pentium processors are now widely available. A Pentium processor is more powerful than a 486 processor which, in turn, is more powerful than a 386.

3. Making recommendations based upon the investigation

After conducting the interviews, Eileen reported back to the managers. She stressed that Remedy would benefit in time and cost savings by rationalising the computerised scheme. At present they are all using the one computer they have got creatively, but it may be that some of the functions could be done better at Head Office. Eileen stressed that their priorities must be to:

● save time;
● generate information;
● have a system which all staff use;
● be conscious of how the system can expand in the future;
● make plans for Remedy as a whole.

In addition, Eileen tabled the following written notes and recommendations.

✳ The first consideration is the installation of an EPOS sale system. It is possible to buy a dedicated cash register system but it does not seem to make economic sense to spend up to £2000 pounds on this if the computer could be extended to provide point of sales facilities. On the other hand, could the computer then be used for anything else? Not only will the EPOS system keep a record of all sales but, by using a suitable program, Remedy will be able to check all stock levels instantly and the system could be made to reorder goods once stock levels have fallen below a predefined point. Some systems could even incorporate ordering but I feel this would entail setting up a computerised network which is too ambitious. However a complete stock control could be implemented locally and transferred to a dedicated warehouse computer system at a later date. A modem would then have to be fitted so that the other branches and the warehouse can be linked up in future.

✳ In the meantime I propose that I further investigate different types of EPOS systems and report back to the next meeting.

✳ It may be that some of the functions could be done better at head office (e.g. personnel details, design of forms, posters, etc.) and this would have the advantage of being done for all the shops.

✳ The data that will be generated needs to be organised into a set of procedures for ensuring accessibility and secure storage. Similar procedures should be applied to current uses of the computer.

✳ Our strategy cannot be to turn everybody into an IT expert. However, some background knowledge would make it easier to spread IT and to motivate staff. Therefore, staff from all the shops should be encouraged to attend general courses at college, provided they can be released from other duties or if they will go in their own time.

> *✱ The hard disk needs to be reorganised. Procedures for saving and labelling data need to be established. Staff need to use common directories and save data according to type. Floppy disk backups are to be made at the end of every session. The labelling must include the date and the version of the file.*

EVIDENCE

Assignment 11 (page 95) provides an opportunity to produce evidence of achievement in ways of using IT. Use every opportunity to evaluate your use of IT throughout the other assignments too.

12 Handling disk files

Gurdip Bola has the following files saved on her floppy disk:

~SPL0541.TMP	GFPLAN2.BMP	SALES1.WKS
~SPL0938.TMP	MAILSHOT.WPS	SALES2.WKS
~SPL1546.TMP	NOTICE1.WRI	STAFF1.WDB
FRANCH1.WRI	PHOTON1.WPS	TEST.
GFPLAN1.BMP	PHOTON2.WPS	

She is worried that there is not enough room left to store any more of her work, so she has asked Eileen MacQuarry for more disks on which to store her data. Eileen has suggested that Gurdip should sort out the files on her existing floppy disk and make a backup of it, as she may not, in fact, need any more disks.

Eileen is concerned about the storage of files on the computer hard disk, as a number of people in the office are now using the computer. There is little co-ordination between the different users on how to document and save files, so files have proliferated and it has become all too easy to lose track of the ones needed.

Eileen has asked Gurdip to set up some appropriate directories on her own floppy disk so that she can become familiar with using directories.

The IT skills Gurdip will use to do this include:

▶ listing files on a disk;
▶ making sub-directories to organise disk files in a logical manner;
▶ copying disk files to relevant directories;
▶ deleting redundant files;
▶ making backup copies.

You can practise these skills by following the steps that Gurdip takes and carrying out the equivalent processes on your own computer.

Practise

? **HELP**
For more examples of MS-DOS functions, turn to page 109.

File Manager

1. Choosing a file management program

The computer in the office uses MS-DOS which is the operating system activated by most IBM-compatible personal computers. (MS-DOS stands for '*Microsoft* Disk Operating System'.) One of the functions of such operating systems is the handling of files and the organisation of directories. The user is not necessarily aware that the operating system is working in the background all the time.

It may be that your computer is not running under MS-DOS. As the differences between systems are minor, however, you should still be able to follow the general principles outlined here.

MS-DOS is often criticised on the grounds that it is too difficult to use. For this reason a number of more 'user friendly' file management programs have emerged, for example *XtreeGold* and *File Manager* – you may be using one of these programs instead of DOS. (Also, many file management tasks can be carried out within other applications.)

MS-DOS is generally known as 'DOS', and it is shown on Gurdip's computer screen as a menu option. When she highlights the name of the program on her screen and presses ENTER, she automatically gets into DOS and the prompt 'C:' is displayed on the screen.

2. Looking at files on a disk

In order to look at the files on her floppy disk, Gurdip needs to change the prompt to a drive that can read floppy disks. In this case it is the A drive. Gurdip keys:

    A: [ENTER]

this changes the prompt 'C:' to 'A:'. Then she keys:

    dir [ENTER]

which lists all the files on the disk in drive A, plus associated information. These files include those which have been created in the process of doing Activities 2 to 7, along with some additional ones that will need deleting.

File name	File extension	the file size (in bytes)	date last saved	time last saved
~SPL0541	TMP	60742	20/02/96	10:13
~SPL0938	TMP	69516	22/03/96	11:14
~SPL1546	TMP	96858	22/03/96	11:14
FRANCH1	WRI	2176	22/03/96	11:14
GFPLAN1	BMP	481078	28/04/96	10:00
GFPLAN2	BMP	481078	28/04/96	10:55
MAILSHOT	WPS	5120	28/04/96	14:05
NOTICE1	WRI	83456	05/05/96	11:10
PHOTON1	WPS	4608	07/05/96	12:00
PHOTON2	WPS	5120	07/05/96	12:30
SALES1	WKS	12110	22/05/96	9:01
SALES2	WKS	12374	22/05/96	9:56
STAFF1	WDB	12288	28/05/96	12:00
TEST		40960	13/06/96	18:11

? **HELP**
If you want more information on file extensions, turn to page 107.

Guidance

A text file is one that is concerned with the presentation of alphabetic characters and numbers. Text files are not designed to display specialised codes and graphic images, therefore you may have difficulties when trying to display some sorts of files

---

? **HELP**
If you need more help with naming files, turn to page 107.

Note that most of these files have an extension added to their name, after the full stop. It is common practice for programs automatically to graft on extensions to filenames. (Extensions can be up to three characters long.)

In addition, there are a number of redundant files. There are three reasons for the existence of redundant files.

- Some temporary files were created when programs were not shut down properly (these are the files that begin with ~ [the tilde sign] and end with the extention TMP).
- Some files have been superseded by later versions (for example, GFPLAN1.BMP has been superseded by GFPLAN2.BMP).
- Some experimental files were created while testing a program (for example the file called TEST).

Gurdip does not recognise the filename TEST and is not sure what is in it, so, to display the contents as a text file, she keys:

```
type TEST [ENTER]
```

If you are uncertain of the contents of a file that is listed, all you need to do to display its contents is key in the command 'type', followed by the relevant filename.

Note that DOS is not case specific. Commands keyed in lower or upper case will be treated in the same way.

Sometimes filenames don't stand the test of time – you may give a file a name that means something to you at the time you create it, but, later on, that name may give you no clue to the file's contents, therefore it now needs a more meaningful name. You can rename files using the 'rename' command. For example, if you key in the command 'rename fred invoice.doc' DOS will rename the file called 'FRED' to a file called 'INVOICE.DOC'.

3. Deleting redundant files

After identifying redundant files, Gurdip needs to delete them.

There are two good reasons for deleting files.

- It saves disk space.
- It prevents the use of obsolete files.

To delete the file called TEST, Gurdip keys:

```
del TEST [ENTER]
```

When you have identified redundant files on a floppy disk, delete them in the same way.

Then, in order to check that the redundant file has been removed, Gurdip keys:

```
dir [ENTER]
```

which lists the files on the relevant directory.

Guidance

The DOS command 'del' is an abbreviation for 'delete'.

Gurdip identified a number of temporary files on her disk by the 'TMP' file extension. These need to be deleted too. This can be done, one by one, using the 'del' command followed by the filename, for example:

```
del ~SPL0541.TMP [ENTER]
```

The problem with this is that each filename has to be individually and exactly entered. A quicker way of deleting all the files in one go, as a batch, would be to use what is known as a 'wild card' facility when specifying the filenames. With this facility you can use an asterisk (*) to represent a character or group of characters in a file name. For example, when Gurdip keys:

```
del *.TMP [ENTER]
```

DOS will delete *all* the files with the 'TMP' extension. If you use a wild card, you must be sure you enter the correct parameters (the parameters are the characters that the filenames have in common with each other – in this case 'TMP').

If you are using a file manager program you can delete files by highlighting them and choosing the DELETE option from the FILE menu.

HELP
If you need more help with wild cards, turn to page 107.

In this file manager program the four temporary files on the A drive have been selected for deletion

Guidance

Be careful! Deleting .TMP files when using *Windows* file manager carries the risk of losing files currently in use and preventing *Windows* from operating correctly in future.

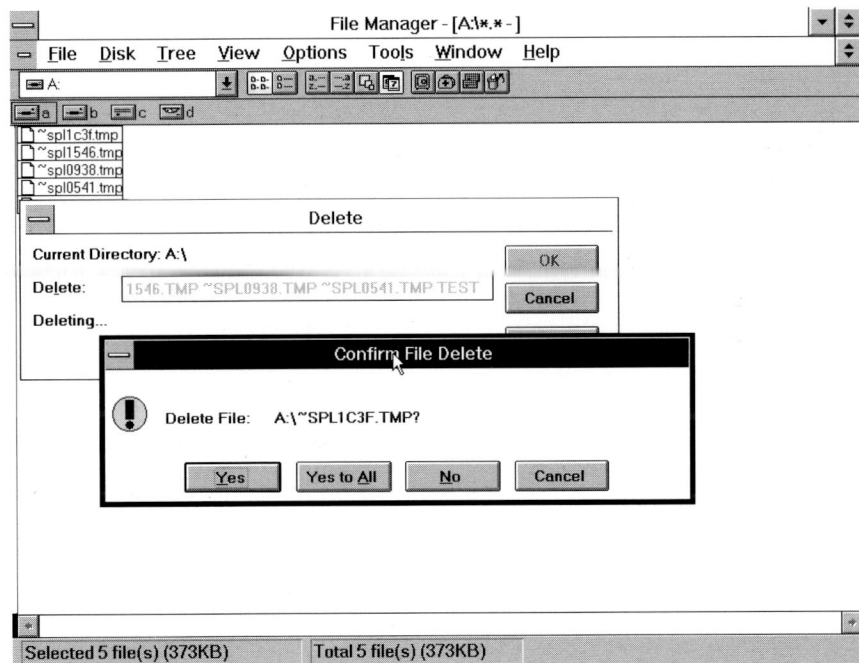

File Manager - [A:*.* -]

File   Disk   Tree   View   Options   Tools   Window   Help

A:

~spl1c3f.tmp
~spl1546.tmp
~spl0938.tmp
~spl0541.tmp

Delete

Current Directory: A:\

Delete: 1546.TMP ~SPL0938.TMP ~SPL0541.TMP TEST

Deleting...

OK

Cancel

Confirm File Delete

Delete File: A:\~SPL1C3F.TMP?

Yes   Yes to All   No   Cancel

Selected 5 file(s) (373KB)   Total 5 file(s) (373KB)

Choose which files you do not need any more and delete them, using a wild card where appropriate.

4. Making sub-directories

Create Directory

Current Directory: A:\

Name: pic

OK

Cancel

Help

Inevitably, over time, the number of files stored on a disk will grow. As with all collections of data, there comes a point when disk files should be categorised, grouped logically, and stored in different sub-directories. Sub-directories are also known as 'folders'.

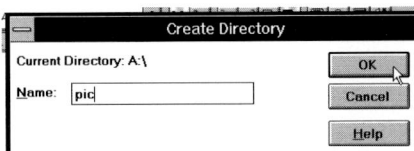

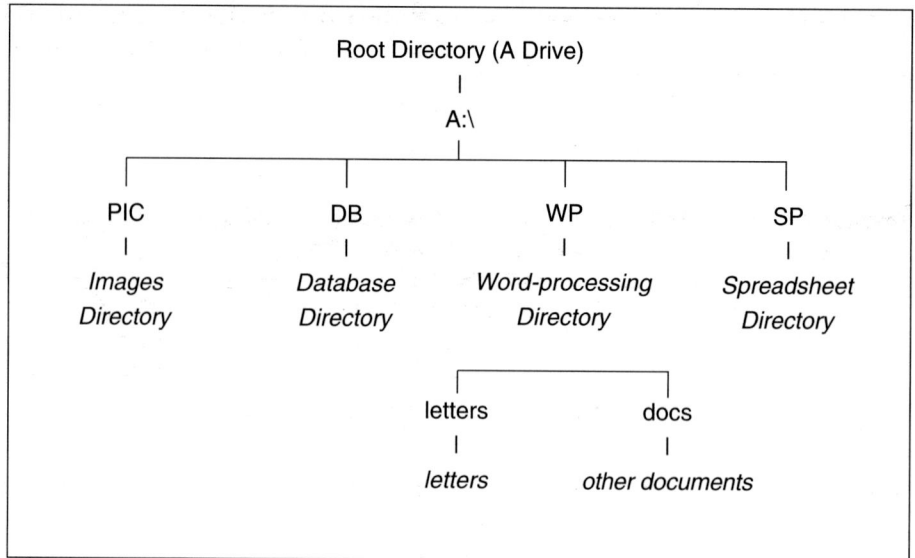

It is possible to have sub-directories within sub-directories. Thus the contents of a floppy disk could be stored in sub-directories (see the directory structure in the figure above).

This arrangement is sometimes called a tree structure. You can see the root (at the top) and, as you go down, the branches develop.

Gurdip uses the 'md' command ('md' stands for 'make directory') to make a sub-directory called 'PIC', in which to store PICtures (i.e. graphical images):

```
md PIC [ENTER]
```

She does the same for spreadsheet files, calling the sub-directory 'SP', for database files ('DB') and for word-processing files ('WP').

Within 'WP' Gurdip wants to make sub-directories for LETTERS and DOCS. To do this she needs to be in the directory from which the sub-directory is to branch out. Gurdip moves from A: (the root directory) to the WP sub-directory by using the change directory command ('cd'):

```
cd WP [ENTER]
```

This takes her into the WP directory. She then keys:

```
md LETTERS [ENTER]

md DOCS [ENTER]
```

Look at your remaining files and set up a structure to arrange them in a logical way, making appropriate sub-directories in which to store them.

If you are using a file manager program, you can make directories by using a CREATE DIRECTORY option from a FILE menu.

5. Copying files

Gurdip's next task is to copy the appropriate files to the appropriate areas.

Guidance

You may wish to go back (up) a directory level. This can be done by keying:
```
cd..
```
which will take you back, one level at a time.

All the word-processing files are to be stored in the directory called 'WP'; all the database files in 'DB'; and so on.

Gurdip uses the 'copy' command:

```
copy PHOTON2.WPS WP\LETTERS [ENTER]
```

which copies the file called 'PHOTON2.WPS' to the LETTERS sub-directory of WP.

When you copy all your files to the appropriate sub-directories, you can check that they have been copied by changing the directory with the 'cd' command and then listing the files using the 'dir' command.

With a file manager program you will find a COPY option on the FILE menu; or you may be able to highlight the files you want to copy and 'drag' them to the relevant sub-directory using the mouse.

6. Write protecting the disk

If you want to stop other people storing things on your disk, you can physically prevent it being written to. On 5.25 inch disks this is done by sticking a metallic tag over the notch. On 3.5 inch disks this is done by moving the plastic tag up to the write protection position.

HELP
For more information about disk sizes and write protection, turn to page 109.

7. Labelling the disk

Disks can easily get mislaid or mixed up, therefore it is important that you put labels on all your disks. (If you are using 5.25 inch disks, write on the label before sticking it on the disk to avoid putting undue pressure on the disk.) The label should show the types of files, dates of saving and the name or initials of the user.

8. Backing up the disk

Disks do get damaged and lost, so it is vital that backup copies of all important files are made. Unlike many large organisations, Remedy has no strict rules about backing up disks, but this is no reason for not making backups. To make a backup, Gurdip makes a copy of her disk. Because the computer at Head Office does not have two identical floppy disk drives, she has to take disks in and out of the same drive. When being copied in this way, disks can become mixed up, therefore it is important to:

● label the disks clearly;
● write protect the source disk.

Gurdip places the source disk ('source disk' is the name given to the disk that contains the information which you want to back up) in drive A and keys:

```
diskcopy a: a:
```

This command copies the contents of the source disk, piece by piece, to a temporary memory in the computer. After copying each piece, DOS asks Gurdip to insert the target disk ('target disk' is the name given to the disk to which you want the information copied). It then transfers the information from the temporary memory to the target disk. Then it asks Gurdip to insert the source disk again, so that it can copy the next piece.

If you are using a file manager program, you should find a COPY DISK option on the DISK menu.

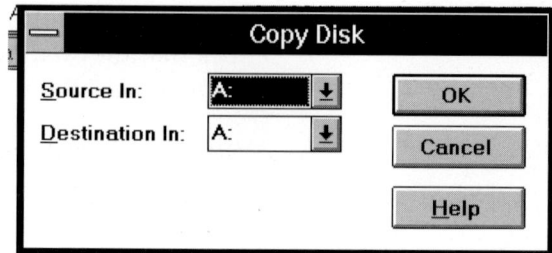

EVIDENCE

Assignment 13 (page 95) provides an opportunity to produce evidence of achievement in file management.

13 Creating a stock file of Oasis products

As the Assistant Manager at the Dover branch, Clare Delaney has been asked to monitor sales of the Oasis health and beauty products. She plans to use a computer program to help to calculate turnover and profit on the Oasis products. Judith Argyle, the Shop Manager, wishes like to see what impact any projected adjustments on prices would make upon revenue.

Converting prices can be a tedious and time-consuming process, so Clare has decided to use a computer to do the conversions.

She starts with a list of products and their order codes. She obtained this information from the Oasis catalogue.

The IT skills she will use to do this include:

▶ setting up the spreadsheet structure;
▶ entering the data;
▶ saving the spreadsheet;
▶ printing it out;
▶ using absolute and relative referencing;
▶ using the spreadsheet to make projections;
▶ reviewing the effectiveness of the spreadsheet.

You can practise these skills by following the steps that Clare takes and carrying out the equivalent processes on your own computer.

Practise

Guidance

A dedicated stock control system or a sophisticated database application would be better for handling a continual flow of incoming delivery notes and sales information. Such packages can be linked to a bar code reader. (See EPOS, page 59 and 61.)

1. Choosing the application

The next decision to be made is what sort of computer application to use. There are stock control applications on the market but Clare and Judith do not have one available. Using a stock control system can be very time consuming, in so far as all transactions have to be computerised. Their immediate requirement is to monitor the sales of Oasis products and to contemplate the impact of changing the prices of these products. Clare thought that the spreadsheet program she already had available would help to meet these needs.

2. Designing the spreadsheet application

In the Dover shop the present system for storing information is to store invoices and delivery notes, on which information is written rather haphazardly. Often, a lot of time is spent searching for one particular piece of paper, and information sometimes gets lost.

To help her to enter the correct labels for the column headings and other data, Clare uses the Oasis product information sheet as the basis for her spreadsheet. This consists of printed pages showing all the products, the codes, and the cost price. Next to the cost price she adds a SOLD column, for which the data have been painstakingly gathered, and the numbers are shown below.

Oasis Product List		Cost Price	Sold	Revenue	Profit
ALMOND OIL BODY LOTION	AOBL	4.00	22		
AZTEC COLOUR BOX	ACB	14.99	5		
TAHITI COLOUR BOX	TCB	14.99	0		
ALPINE COLOUR BOX	ACB	14.99	2		
OCEAN JEWELS EYE COLOURS	OJEC	4.99	6		
FOREST SECRETS EYE COLOURS	FSEC	4.99	1		
DESERT FLOWERS EYE COLOURS	DFEC	4.99	18		
PAPRIKA LIP COLOURS	PLC	4.99	25		
CINNAMON LIP COLOURS	CLC	4.99	10		
JASMINE LIP COLOURS	JLC	4.99	22		
NATURAL KELP SHAMPOO	NKS	3.99	16		
NATURAL KELP CONDITIONER	NKC	2.99	18		
PASSION FRUIT BODY LOTION	PFBL	3.50	22		
APPLE MINT FOOT LOTION	AMFL	1.75	18		
CRUSHED APRICOT MOISTURISER	CAM	3.99	34		
BANANA FACIAL WASH CREAM	BFWC	1.90	10		
PAPAYA DEEP CLEANSER	PDC	2.10	46		
PINEAPPLE SCRUB DEFOLIANT	PSD	2.75	27		
LEMON GRASS ASTRINGENT WASH	LGAW	1.75	22		
WHITE GRAPE SKIN TONIC	WGST	1.50	24		

3. Opening the spreadsheet and entering labels and column headings

Guidance

In this activity, it is assumed that you already know a little about using spreadsheets. If you don't, turn to Activity 10 (page 56) and look at pages 112–16 in the Help Section.

Guidance

It is clear that the products column needs to be widened. If you need a reminder on how to do this, look at Activity 6, page 38. Tables of numbers can look ungainly if the columns are too wide and if the widths are irregular, therefore it is usually appropriate to try to reduce the space occupied by the column titles. Provided they are clear, abbreviations are perfectly acceptable in column headings.

Clare chooses the spreadsheet application from the main menu. When she is presented with a blank spreadsheet on screen, Clare positions the cursor in cell A1 and keys in the text 'Oasis Products'. She then goes to the next but one cell on the right (C1) and keys in 'Sales for the first 13 weeks'. The second row (2) is left empty – this is done to improve the appearance of the spreadsheet. In cell A3 Clare enters 'Mark up =' and in cell B3 she enters $=\frac{1}{3}$. (Note that although the mark up is one third, the computer shows this number in decimal format.)

Clare enters the column headings in the cells along row 6. She emboldens the headings. This is what the screen looks like once she has done so.

B3		=1/3				
	A		**B**	**C**	**D**	**E**	**F**
1	Oasis Products			Sales for the first 13 weeks		
2						
3	Mark up =		0.33			
4						
5						
6	Products		Cost Price	Shop Price	Sold	Revenue	Profit

Use this data, or your own, to enter column headings. Remember to make sure that their meaning is clear.

4. Entering the products, cost prices and quantities sold

Now Clare enters the appropriate data from the annotated price list into the cells under the column headings. Strictly speaking, there is no need to put in all the information about the products. Clare decides to use the products' names and not their codes. This is because the names are more meaningful than the codes, and they do not take up too much space.

Guidance

Using codes can save having to enter a lot of information. Unnecessarily large cells can waste space and can be a nuisance both when entering data and when printing reports in which one is trying to show a lot of information on the same page.

	A	B	C	D	E	F
1	Oasis Products		Sales for the first 13 weeks			
2						
3	Mark up =	0.33				
4						
5						
6	Products	Cost Price	Shop Price	Sold	Revenue	Profit
7						
8	ALMOND OIL BODY LOTION	3.00		22		
9	AZTEC COLOUR BOX	11.24		5		
10	TAHITI COLOUR BOX	11.24		0		
11	ALPINE COLOUR BOX	11.24		2		
12	OCEAN JEWELS EYE COLOURS	3.74		6		
13	FOREST SECRETS EYE COLOURS	3.74		1		
14	DESERT FLOWERS EYE COLOURS	3.74		18		
15	PAPRIKA LIP COLOURS	3.74		25		
16	CINNAMON LIP COLOURS	3.74		10		
17	JASMINE LIP COLOURS	3.74		22		
18	NATURAL KELP SHAMPOO	2.99		16		
19	NATURAL KELP CONDITIONER	2.24		18		
20	PASSION FRUIT BODY LOTION	2.63		22		
21	APPLE MINT FOOT LOTION	1.31		18		
22	CRUSHED APRICOT MOISTURISER	2.99		34		
23	BANANA FACIAL WASH CREAM	1.43		10		
24	PAPAYA DEEP CLEANSER	1.58		46		
25	PINEAPPLE SCRUB DEFOLIANT	2.06		27		
26	LEMON GRASS ASTRINGENT WASH	1.31		22		
27	WHITE GRAPE SKIN TONIC	1.13		24		

Move the cursor down the columns and key in the appropriate data. Note that the data in column A is textual but that in remaining columns it is numerical.

5. Saving the spreadsheet

Clare now saves the document. When you save your spreadsheet, remember to give it a name that reflects its purpose – Clare calls hers 'OASIS1'.

6. Entering the formula to generate the retail prices

? HELP
You will find that the symbols used for formulas vary from spreadsheet to spreadsheet, so the start of your formula may need to be a '+' or '@'. Find out about this from your manual or on-screen help. If you need help with formulas, turn to page 113.

Using formulas in a spreadsheet ensures that calculations can be automatically updated as numerical data is changed. To mark up the cost prices in column B by one third, Clare needs to insert an appropriate formula in column C under the 'Shop Price' heading. The formula she inserts has to add on one third to the prices in column B. The spreadsheet needs to know that this entry is a formula. This can be done by starting the formula with a symbol, in this case an equals sign (=). In this case the shop price for *Almond Oil Body Lotion* can be generated by using the formula =B8+B8*1/3. There are other ways of doing this.

7. Setting an absolute reference and replicating the formula

Guidance

In Activity 6 (see page 39) you should have copied formulas using relative referencing.

While the entry in C8 works, there is one drawback to it. Clare knows that, at a later stage, Judith would like to try changing the 'mark up' factor, to see how revenue and profit might be affected. In order to do this all the entries in cells C8 to C27 would have to be changed manually. It would be much better to define just one cell – cell B3 – as the key cell which contains the mark up ratio. The result of changing the content of this cell should automatically adjust all the calculations which entail the use of the 'mark up' formula. When she enters the formula, however, Clare needs to set any reference to cell B3 as an 'absolute reference'.

In a formula, an absolute reference is a reference that remains constant no matter where you are replicating the formula. The reference to 'mark up' in cell B3 is a good example. Thus, the first time Clare refers to cell B3 in a formula this ensures that the reference is absolute. To do this Clare inserts a $ sign in front of each part of the appropriate cell reference, so that B3 becomes B3.

C8	=B8*B3+B8		
	A	B	C
1	Oasis Products		Sales for the first 13
2			
3	Mark up =	=1/3	
4			
5			
6	Products	Cost Price	Shop Price	Sold
7			
8	ALMOND OIL BODY LOTION	3	=B8*B3+B8	2?

Entering the formula, with absolute references, into cell C8

6	Shop Price
7	
8	=C8*B3+C8
9	=C9*B4+C9
10	=C10*B5+C10
11	=C11*B6+C11
12	=C12*B7+C12
13	=C13*B8+C13
14	=C14*B9+C14
15	

Relative referencing

6	Shop Price
7	
8	=C8*B3+C8
9	=C9*B3+C9
10	=C10*B3+C10
11	=C11*B3+C11
12	=C12*B3+C12
13	=C13*B3+C13
14	=C14*B3+C14
15	

Absolute referencing

Clare replicates the formula to the other cells in column C by highlighting the cell to be copied (C8), extending the highlight down to include the cells she wants to fill (C9 to C27) and then choosing the FILL DOWN option from the EDIT menu. Using this, she replicates (copies) the contents of the selected cell down to the remaining cells in column C.

8. Calculating revenue and profit

As the number sold has already been entered, the revenue is easy to calculate. It is the number multiplied by the retail price. Clare enters the formula =C8*D8 in cell E8. She checks that the right sum is generated. As the answer 88.00 appears correct, she concludes that the formula is sound and replicates this formula into cells E9 to E27.

There are a number of ways of calculating profit. Clare does this by subtracting from the revenue the number of items sold multiplied by the cost price. She enters the formula =E8 -(D9*B9). She then replicates this into cells F9 to F27.

See if you can do the same.

9. The totals for the quarter

A total is needed at the bottom of the Revenue and Profit columns (in a new 'Total' row – row 28). Clare does this by entering the formula '=SUM(E8:E27)' into cell E28. She then replicates this formula into cell F28.

The spreadsheet calculates these totals and the figures 1228.28 and 307.07 should appear in cells E28 and F28.

If your total is different, carefully check all the entries in all the columns. Check that the data you have entered is the same as on the source document – that is, the data shown on the Oasis product sheet shown on page 000. If your data entry appears to be correct, then check your formula. Inaccuracies can be very costly.

31	Date : 25/6/96
32	
33	Saved as Oasis2

10. Date stamping and printing the spreadsheet

It is all too easy to lose track of the different versions of spreadsheets, therefore it is good practice to store the date on the spreadsheet. This is

Guidance

At this stage you might want to try to ensure that your spreadsheet does not take up too much 'empty space' by fine-tuning the layout (e.g. column widths). It is advisable to have the majority of the columns the same width – a lot of uneven column widths can be very distracting.

sometimes known as 'date stamping'. Clare decides to insert the date in the bottom left-hand corner. When she has done so, she adds the cell name.

Your program may not format dates in the same way. Find out how it is done, insert the date into your spreadsheet and then print it out.

Before printing, Clare selects the PRINT PREVIEW option from the FILE menu to make sure that the spreadsheet fits on to one page.

If your spreadsheet program has this facility, try it. Your spreadsheet should look something like this.

Guidance

Some spreadsheets come with an option that lets you scale a worksheet so that it will fit on a printed page. Using such an option will mean that any manual page breaks will be ignored.

Oasis Products			Sales for the first 13 weeks	
Mark up =			0.33	

Products	Cost Price	Shop Price	Sold	Revenue	Profit
ALMOND OIL BODY LOTION	3.00	4.00	22	88.00	22.00
AZTEC COLOUR BOX	11.24	14.99	5	74.95	18.74
TAHITI COLOUR BOX	11.24	14.99	0	0.00	0.00
ALPINE COLOUR BOX	11.24	14.99	2	29.98	7.50
OCEAN JEWELS EYE COLOURS	3.74	4.99	6	29.94	7.49
FOREST SECRETS EYE COLOURS	3.74	4.99	1	4.99	1.25
DESERT FLOWERS EYE COLOURS	3.74	4.99	18	89.82	22.46
PAPRIKA LIP COLOURS	3.74	4.99	25	124.75	31.19
CINNAMON LIP COLOURS	3.74	4.99	10	49.90	12.48
JASMINE LIP COLOURS	3.74	4.99	22	109.78	27.45
NATURAL KELP SHAMPOO	2.99	3.99	16	63.84	15.96
NATURAL KELP CONDITIONER	2.24	2.99	18	53.82	13.46
PASSION FRUIT BODY LOTION	2.63	3.50	22	77.00	19.25
APPLE MINT FOOT LOTION	1.31	1.75	18	31.50	7.88
CRUSHED APRICOT MOISTURISER	2.99	3.99	34	135.66	33.92
BANANA FACIAL WASH CREAM	1.43	1.90	10	19.00	4.75
PAPAYA DEEP CLEANSER	1.58	2.10	46	96.60	24.15
PINEAPPLE SCRUB DEFOLIANT	2.06	2.75	27	74.25	18.56
LEMON GRASS ASTRINGENT WASH	1.31	1.75	22	38.50	9.63
WHITE GRAPE SKIN TONIC	1.13	1.50	24	36.00	9.00
				1228.28	307.07

Date : 25/6/96

Saved as Oasis2

Guidance

Some spreadsheets have special facilities that make it possible to generate a date automatically. While this can be useful – it saves you having to look up the date – it can also be finicky. You must also check to see whether the date is changed every time the spreadsheet is used.

11. Saving the spreadsheet securely

Putting the date on the spreadsheet helps Clare to keep track of files. Another method of keeping track of different versions is to sequence the file names. For this reason, Clare saves her final version as 'OASIS2'.

There are other reasons for saving in this way, such as:

● An earlier version may be known to be doing a job well, whereas the latest version may still need to be tested. It is useful, therefore, to keep a copy of both versions. It is particularly important to keep earlier versions if your spreadsheet design is fairly complicated.

● Sometimes a document may be corrupted when being saved. Using different names means that you will not have to start again from scratch if this happens.

12. Templates

Guidance

Some spreadsheets have customised template facilities. These allow you to create a spreadsheet with all the formulas, functions and formatting that you normally use, and then to save the file as a template.

When Clare was happy with what she had done, she showed a copy of the spreadsheet to Judith Argyle, the Shop Manager. Judith made the point that it seemed that a lot of effort had gone into computerising a task that is relatively easily done without a computer. It is certainly true that one-off calculations can be done much more quickly with a calculator. However, the spreadsheet has the advantage of providing a *permanent* record of the sales.

The spreadsheet was also valuable because it could be used for the next quarter and, furthermore, it could be used by other branches of Remedy. This could be done by setting it up as a template, keeping just the headings and formulas, and saving it under an appropriate name, such as 'MASTER'. Then, all one would need to do is to open 'MASTER' and input the appropriate data.

13. Using the spreadsheet to make projections

Judith was keen to explore another facility. She wanted to know what effect changing the mark-up percentage would have on the profits. By using the spreadsheet facility, she and Clare were able to look at the results of different mark ups, such as 20% and 50%.

Judith was quick to point out that the spreadsheet failed to take into account the fact that changes in prices ought to result in adjustments to the numbers of items sold. This was one weakness of the spreadsheet.

It could be further improved by adding a column for items in stock, thereby calculating the value of the Oasis products actually on the shelves.

EVIDENCE

Assignment 10 (page 94) provides an opportunity to produce evidence of achievement in using spreadsheets at LEVEL 3.

14 Communicating with other computers

Guidance

EPOS stands for **E**lectronic **P**oint **O**f **S**ales and is a system of gathering information regarding sales and stock levels. For further information, refer to Activity 11 on page 58.

Almost all products seem to be bar-coded nowadays so it makes sense to use a bar-code reader at checkout tills to log the items sold. The bar-code reader could form one part of an EPOS system. Eileen wants to link a bar-code reader to the new computer Remedy is planning to buy for the Dover branch. Not only will the EPOS system keep a record of all sales but, by using a suitable program, Remedy will be able to check all stock levels instantly and the system could be made to reorder goods once stock levels have fallen below a pre-defined point.

Eileen is cautious about spending large amounts of money on EPOS software that may prove inappropriate. She decided to find out more about EPOS systems and to do this by using her computer to search other computers for information about EPOS programs. Her computer has a modem which allows it to communicate with remote computer systems. She can also access the Internet which will allow her to download programs and save them on disk so that they can be tested out back at Head Office.

The IT skills she will use to do this include:

► accessing a remote source;
► searching for information;
► downloading information.

You can practise these skills by following the steps that Eileen takes and carrying out the equivalent processes on a computer that has a remote link.

Practise

Guidance

CompuServe, AOL and *Delphi* are 'closed' network providers. Through them you can gain access to the Internet and also access to their own mini-networks which are more organised and better regulated than the Internet. The 'closed' networks are also easier to use and find your way around in. There are also 'gateway' providers (such as *Demon*). These companies provide access to the Internet only, not to the closed networks. (If you subscribe to a gateway provider, you can e-mail users in closed networks but you can't access or download information.)

HELP
For more help on the Internet, turn to page 125.

1. Logging on

To be able to log on to the Internet Eileen has to have an e-mail address which she will get by subscribing to a company that provides access to the Internet. One of these companies, and the one that Eileen subscribes to, is called CompuServe. On screen, Eileen is presented with a variety of icons representing all the external services that the computer can access. She chooses the icon for CompuServe. The computer you use may have a different icon if a different company is used to access the Internet.

When Eileen chooses the *CompuServe* icon, the computer automatically dials up the host system (i.e. *CompuServe*). While it is doing this, the lights on the modem flicker. When the computer gets through, the host system asks for the user's identity and password. In Eileen's case there is no need to key this in because this is sent automatically.

When the password is accepted, the connection is made and the host system's welcome screen is displayed:

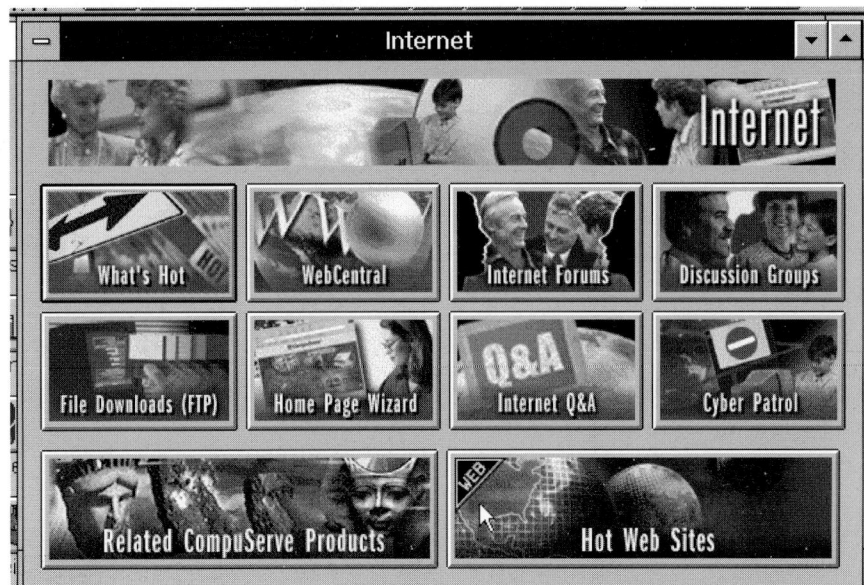

2 Browsing

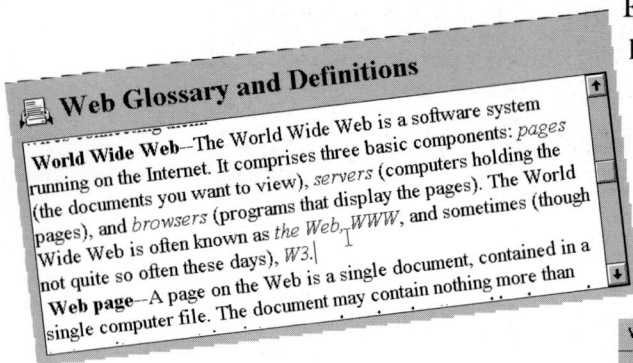

Eileen chooses the Web Central option which allows her to look at pages from the World Wide Web, which is part of the Internet.

First of all, Eileen decides to feel her way around the system and look for areas of interest that are related to her task. Eileen is presented with various search engine and she chooses a well-known one called Yahoo. Eileen then starts some preliminary searches to find out if there are any programs related to EPOS systems. To do this she enters the key word EPOS. She finds eleven apparent matches.

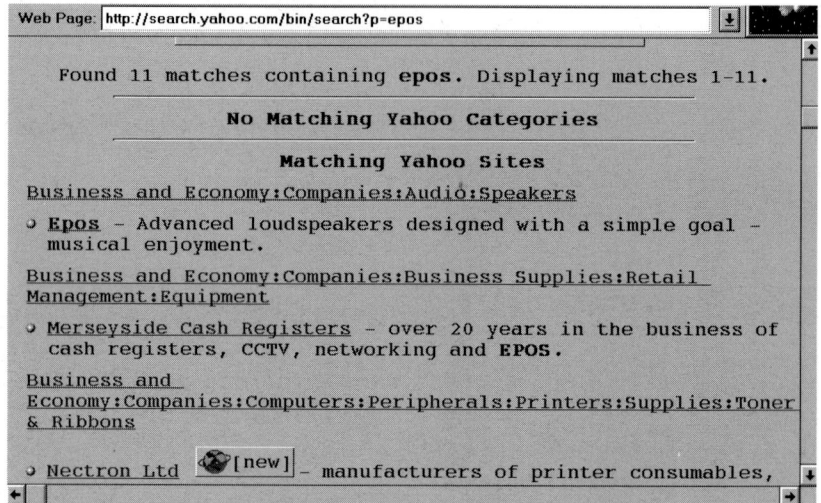

Web Glossary and Definitions

World Wide Web—The World Wide Web is a software system running on the Internet. It comprises three basic components: *pages* (the documents you want to view), *servers* (computers holding the pages), and *browsers* (programs that display the pages). The World Wide Web is often known as *the Web*, *WWW*, and sometimes (though not quite so often these days), *W3*.

Web page—A page on the Web is a single document, contained in a single computer file. The document may contain nothing more than

```
Web Page: http://search.yahoo.com/bin/search?p=epos

Found 11 matches containing epos. Displaying matches 1-11.

              No Matching Yahoo Categories

                 Matching Yahoo Sites
Business and Economy:Companies:Audio:Speakers
  Epos - Advanced loudspeakers designed with a simple goal -
  musical enjoyment.
Business and Economy:Companies:Business Supplies:Retail
Management:Equipment
  Merseyside Cash Registers - over 20 years in the business of
  cash registers, CCTV, networking and EPOS.
Business and
Economy:Companies:Computers:Peripherals:Printers:Supplies:Toner
& Ribbons
  Nectron Ltd  [new] - manufacturers of printer consumables,
```

Eileen clicks the highlighted areas on the screen (these are sometimes known as 'hotspots' or 'hyperlinks') to investigate them further. This browsing on the Internet is often known as 'surfing'.

3. Finding programs

Eileen found nothing which seemed particularly relevant so she decided to try some other search engines: see below

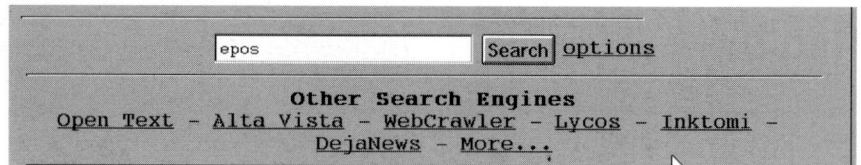

```
epos                    Search options

              Other Search Engines
Open Text - Alta Vista - WebCrawler - Lycos - Inktomi -
                DejaNews - More...
```

She finds a section, within CompuServe, which specifically describes software which can be downloaded. She tries keying in 'computer based' and the computer lists three available programs.

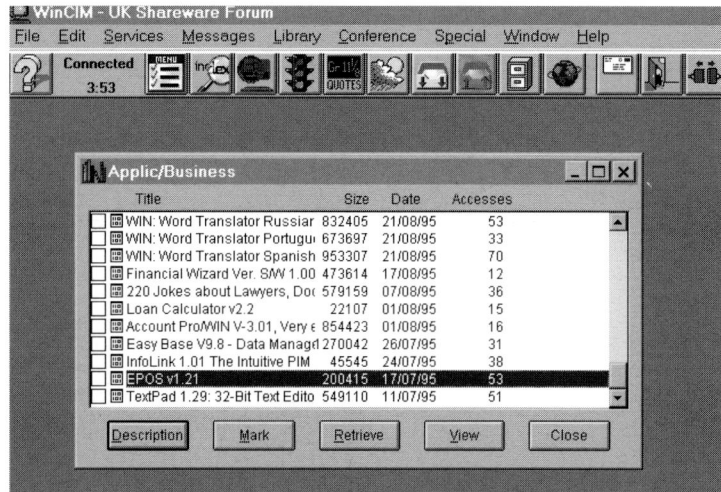

From the list, Eileen finds a program called EPOS V1.21, which she thinks might do the job. When she selects it, more information is displayed about it.

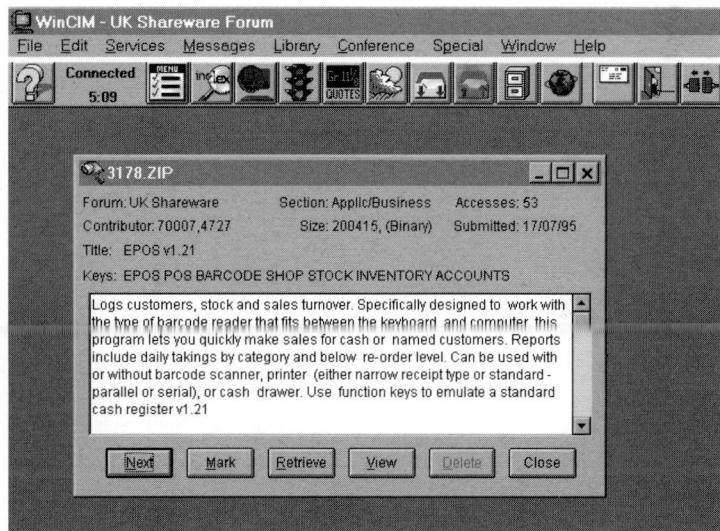

4. Downloading the program

It might be very helpful to study this program so Eileen decides to download it to take back to Enterprise House.

From the FILE FINDER option on the screen, Eileen selects the DOWNLOAD option and specifies that she wants the *EPOS V1.21* program saved on to a floppy disk in the A drive.

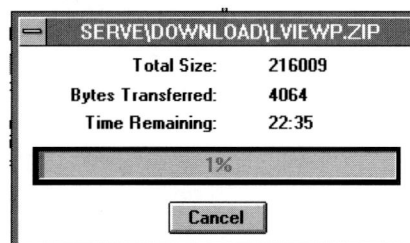

5. Testing the program

Eileen decides to run *EPOS V1.21* to see if it lives up to its promise. However, she finds that she cannot run it immediately because it has been downloaded in a compressed format. This means that files take up less space and can be downloaded more quickly. To restore the file so that the program can be run, it needs to be expanded. The instructions for 'unzipping' programs had been downloaded as a text file accompanying the program and Eileen follows the instructions accordingly.

6. Paying for the program

Having decided to try out the program at Enterprise House, Eileen now needs to find out the cost of the program. She finds the answer within the program's help screens. While looking through them, she also finds that *EPOS V1.21* is categorised as shareware. The help screens display information about shareware, explaining how it works. Here is an extract.

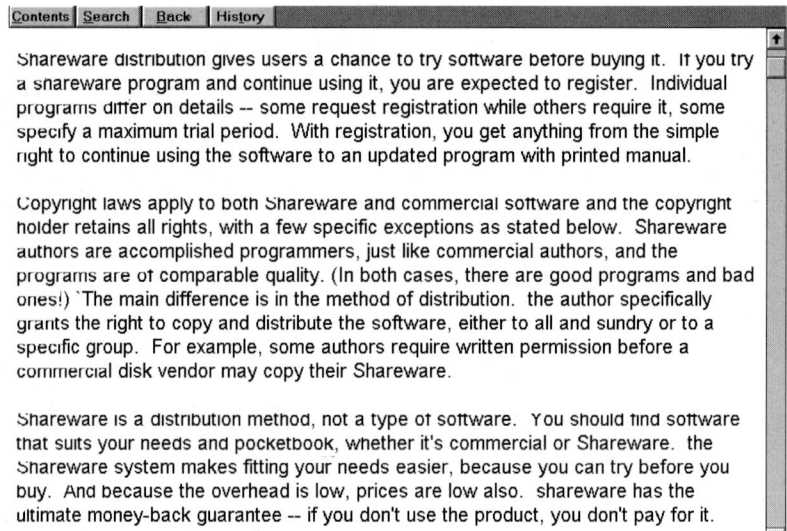

Contents	Search	Back	History	

Shareware distribution gives users a chance to try software before buying it. If you try a shareware program and continue using it, you are expected to register. Individual programs differ on details -- some request registration while others require it, some specify a maximum trial period. With registration, you get anything from the simple right to continue using the software to an updated program with printed manual.

Copyright laws apply to both Shareware and commercial software and the copyright holder retains all rights, with a few specific exceptions as stated below. Shareware authors are accomplished programmers, just like commercial authors, and the programs are of comparable quality. (In both cases, there are good programs and bad ones!) The main difference is in the method of distribution. the author specifically grants the right to copy and distribute the software, either to all and sundry or to a specific group. For example, some authors require written permission before a commercial disk vendor may copy their Shareware.

Shareware is a distribution method, not a type of software. You should find software that suits your needs and pocketbook, whether it's commercial or Shareware. the Shareware system makes fitting your needs easier, because you can try before you buy. And because the overhead is low, prices are low also. shareware has the ultimate money-back guarantee -- if you don't use the product, you don't pay for it.

EVIDENCE
Assignment 9 (page 94) provides an opportunity to produce evidence of attainment in communicating with other computers.

15 Customising the staff database

Eileen MacQuarry likes the staff database but thinks more could be done with it. She asks Gurdip to see if it is possible to calculate members of staff's ages. She would like to be able to produce more specialised reports, such as one which shows only staff names and telephone numbers, grouped according to the shops they work at. She is also worried about the confidentiality of the system.

The IT skills Gurdip will use to do this include:

▶ re-structuring the database;
▶ generating calculations;
▶ preparing and printing customised reports;
▶ ensuring security and confidentiality.

You can practise these skills by following the steps that Gurdip takes and carrying out the equivalent processes on your own computer.

Practise

1. Inserting extra fields

Using the FILE menu, Gurdip opens the existing database, called STAFF1. She decides to insert two new fields. The first one is called DATE, the second one is AGE.

Gurdip does this by viewing the data in table format and by marking the top of the first free column, on the right-hand edge of the table. She selects EDIT and the FIELD NAME option.

Post Code: |DO7 8TD|

Telephone: |01304 4

Date of Birth: |23/03/6

Shop: |D|

Insert Field

Type a width that will best fit your entries. Type a new height if you want a multi-line field.

Name: |Date|
Width: |20|
Height: |1|

OK
Cancel
Help

She calls it DATE and specifies that the format should be date. She then does the same for AGE and sets a field length of 2.

She could have done this in LIST view by placing her cursor on the place on the form and selecting the Insert Field option.

2. Calculating the date

Many databases will allow you to perform calculations. In this case the age can be derived by means of applying calculation facilities. First, Gurdip has to enter the date into the Date field. She does this in LIST view by entering the current date (28/06/96) into the first record and then copying this down.

In the Age field in the first record, Gurdip enters the following definition =Date-Date of Birth/365 which will generate the age in years. (The answer in days must be divided by 365 to convert it to years.)

In order to ensure that this is displayed as a whole number Gurdip formats the AGE field as a whole number by using the INT function. INT stands for integer which is another way of saying a whole number.

Guidance

Many packages have a facility which allows them to generate the date automatically by reading the date stored in the computer. On Gurdip's database defining the field content as =NOW() would have done this. Some other databases have CURRENT functions which serve a similar purpose. Use of this type of function would have eliminated the need to have a field showing the current date.

(Another way of achieving this effect is by specifying no decimal places when specifying the number format.)

Guidance

Strictly speaking this formula does not take into account leap years. A better calculation would be to divide the number of days by 365.25 but even this is not absolutely precise. It may be that your package contains more sophisticated facilities which can counter this possible source of error.

=INT((Today's Date-Date

=INT((NOW()-Date of Bi

This shows two different ways of achieving the same purpose

Most databases will allow calculations to be done upon related fields, although you may need to look in the manual, or ask your tutor, to find out how this can be done. Once you have got it to work, make sure that you write down the method you used.

3. Customised report

The standard printout displays more information than people normally need. When using a database, people usually want specific information, such as names, telephone numbers, branches where they work, but not the full addresses. Gurdip has decided, therefore, to prepare a customised report. She does this by selecting the NEW REPORT facility from the TOOLS menu. She then chooses which fields she wishes to include in the report and, in this case, selects First Name, Surname and Telephone number.

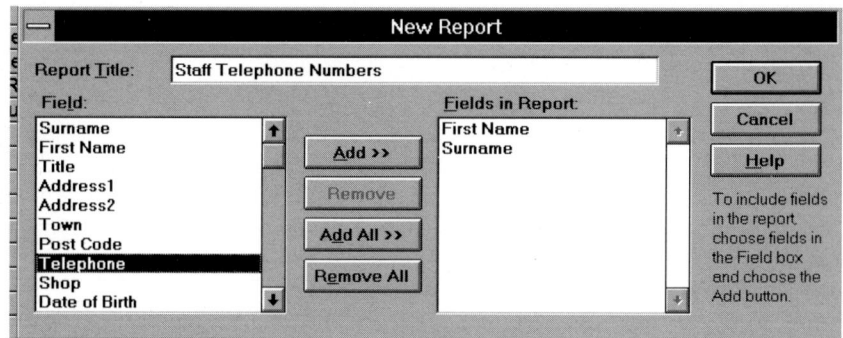

Database report facilities will often allow you to generate statistics. In this case, Gurdip decided to generate another report showing the ages and the average age of the staff.

She also uses the COUNT facility to count the number of staff on this list (she signifies that she wants to count the first names). Both of these items are to be placed at the bottom of the report, under the appropriate column.

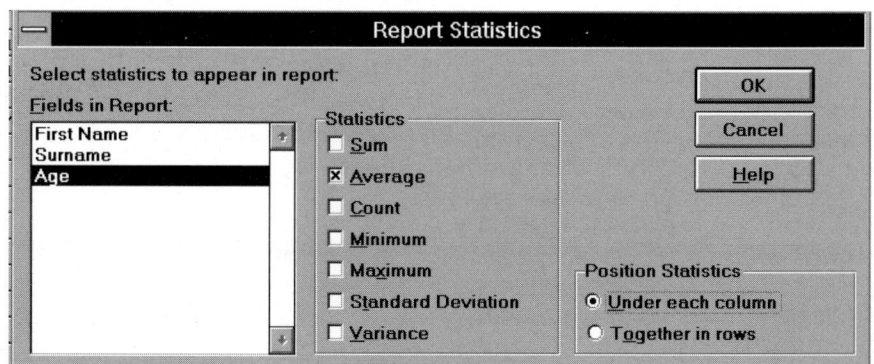

4. Headers and footers

Then, from the VIEW menu, Gurdip selects HEADERS & FOOTERS and inserts the relevant special codes for inserting page numbers, etc. Below, you can see exactly what she specified.

	A	B	C	D	E
Title					
Headings	First Name	Surname	Age		
Headings					
Record	=First Name	=Surname	=Age		
Summary					
Summary	Number of Staff:		=COUNT(SL		
Summary	Average Age:		=AVG(Age)		

Headers and Footers

Header: &l&f&c&d   OK

Footer: Cancel

☐ No header on 1st page   ☐ Use header and   Help
☐ No footer on 1st page   footer paragraphs

This is what the completed report now looks like.

STAFF2A.WDB   28/06/96

First Name	Surname	Age
Mark	Hartshorn	30
Judith	Argyle	33
Sukhinder	Kaushal	18
David	Hucker	58
Shirley	Squires	25
Rosemary	Fraser-Hardy	31
Keith	Lysencko	27
Linford	Andrews	34
Jef	Robinson	42
Clare	Delaney	35
Harry	Dawe	50
Catherine	Hinds	32

Number of Staff:	12
Average Age:	35

5. Security

The database program does not have the facility to set passwords. Gurdip thinks that people are unlikely to want to use it for malicious or illegal purposes but it would be best if there was a password.

What do you think? See if you can activate a password system on your database.

6. Saving the file and shutting down the program in the correct sequence

Many database programs save the data automatically upon leaving the program, provided the program is exited properly. Gurdip needs to make sure that the latest version of the file is saved so she saves it using the name STAFF2.

7. Evaluating the report functions

The reporting facilities become very important when there is a large amount of information available or when the information to be displayed is to go to people who are not familiar with the subject. Hence, there is a need for customised 'user friendly' reports.

Gurdip decides to spend a lot of time looking at the other facilities which are available, to see which might become useful in the future. For example, she finds out that it is possible to group data under common sub-categories, such as the branch name. Gurdip realises that this can be avoided by selecting what, in her program, is called the break check box. Other databases will have other ways of selecting and displaying groups.

Explore the reporting facilities on your system. You may well find it more effective to integrate the data into a word-processing or desktop publishing program, as is done in the next activity.

EVIDENCE
Assignments 4 and 5 (page 92) provide an opportunity to produce evidence of achievement in using storage systems and inputting information, editing and organising information, and selecting and using formats for presenting information.

16 Compiling a report

Eileen MacQuarry at Head Office wants Judith Argyle, the manager of the Dover branch, to compile a report on the last three months of trading, using various documents that have already been generated, such as:

- a spreadsheet showing the cash and credit income (SALES2 in Activity 6);
- a 3D bar graph showing the cash and credit income (see Activity 7);
- a line graph showing the income (see Activity 7);
- a copy of the Oasis display poster (see Activity 4);
- a breakdown of the Oasis sales (see Activity 13).

Judith knows that most of the information is already stored and that most of the work will consist of presenting already prepared information in a combined format.

The IT skills she will use to do this include:

▶ locating already prepared information;
▶ combining this with additional text;
▶ presenting combined information in a suitable format, using page numbering and a consistent layout.

You can practise these skills by following the steps that Judith takes and carrying out the equivalent processes on your own computer.

。 Practise

1. The report structure

This is a copy of the notes that Eileen has made with reference to the structure of the report.

Cover page: Heading and table of contents eg

Report on Dover for January to April 1996

Cash and credit income   page 2

3 D Chart for Income   page 3

Line graph showing Income   page 4

Breakdown of the sales for the Oasis products   page 5

Publicity Poster for Oasis products   page 6

At the bottom of page one show your name, status and the date of the report.

The cover page is not to be numbered. The other pages are, as shown above. Adjust all the images so that they are centred across the pages, and try, within reason, to enlarge them so that we do not have too much empty (white) space.

Judith decides to use a word-processing program which is part of an integrated suite of software. This makes it easy to include material created in the spreadsheet and graphics applications.

You do not have to use a word-processing program when you key in the text. A desktop publishing program will serve the purpose just as well. However, it does help if the text is stored in an environment (such as *Windows*) in which data can be easily transferred from one application to another.

2. Setting up the front page

When she gets into the word-processing program, Judith looks at the report specification. The first line of the report serves as both the title for

? HELP
Arial is one example of a plain sans-serif font that will stand out at a distance. For more information about fonts and styles, turn to pages 103 and 104.

the cover page and for the report. Judith keys in the title text. She decides that this heading should be sufficiently large to spread across most of the line and, in order to make it stand out, she uses a simpler sans-serif font. She selects 18 as the type size and Arial as her font style.

Judith also decides to centre the title. This is how it will appear:

Report on Dover for January to April 1996

You can also do this now. You do not have to create a title using exactly the same facilities – have a look round your program and create a title in a style that you think is appropriate.

Judith then enters the references to each section and the page references. These page references have to be lined up. She does this by using the tabulation facility (usually known as 'tabs'). Thus, for example, on the line which reads:

Cash and credit income	page 2

she presses the TAB key before the word 'page'. This shifts the following text, in this case page 2, up to a predefined line. As this is not far enough over to the right, Judith decides to change the default setting to 12 cm. On her program the TABS setting is found within the VIEW option.

Judith decides that it would be better to embolden and enlarge the last three lines on the cover page and pull them down to the bottom of the page. She feels that this gives the report a more balanced look. This is how her front page appears.

Guidance

More sophisticated programmes will allow you to call up already defined styles automatically, and apply them to selected text.

Guidance

More sophisticated programs will allow you to generate a table of contents automatically. One advantage of the table of contents is that it will automatically detect the page numbers and line up these references on the right-hand side. Understandably, the table of contents is derived from the existing contents, therefore this is the last thing to be prepared. Furthermore, the program needs to know what items are to be included in the contents list. This can be done by distinguishing the text, and by identifying it as a particular style which can be recognised by the table of contents facility. This will entail identifying a heading at the top of every page. If your program allows you to do so, try using the table Of contents facilities.

Set out your own version accordingly.

Judith saves the document as REPORT1.

3. Preparing and importing the spreadsheet data

Now Judith needs to bring the relevant spreadsheet data into the document. As this is to be done on a new page of text, she selects the NEW PAGE option from the INSERT menu. The spreadsheet is now to be placed at the top of this page.

Guidance

This is sometimes known as page break.

Then Judith opens the spreadsheet file (saved as SALES2 in Activity 6), and clicks on the COPY icon, highlighting all the relevant spreadsheet data to copy.

	A	B	
1	Weeks	CASH	
2			
3	Wk 1	5917.60	
4	Wk 2	6736.86	
5	Wk 3	4500.93	
6	Wk 4	4003.68	
7	Wk 5	2579.76	
8	Wk 6	4404.04	
9	Wk 7	2837.73	

The COPY menu on your spreadsheet may require you to specify the range of cells you want to copy the formula to by keying them in, rather than highlighting them.

Judith then carries this data across into the word-processing program. To do this she gets back into the word-processed document by selecting it from the WINDOW menu on the toolbar. She selects the document REPORT1 from the WINDOW menu.

Guidance

On many spreadsheets it is possible to highlight the whole spreadsheet simply by clicking on the top left-hand corner of the grid, see below:

You may also be able to insert the spreadsheet data as a linked file to the word-processed document so that if the source data changes, the word-processed document will be up-dated.

When she is returned to the word-processed document, Judith places the cursor where she wants the spreadsheet data to be inserted and selects PASTE from the EDIT menu. The data that she copied from the spreadsheet is then automatically inserted at that point.

There are different ways of importing extracts from spreadsheets, and it may be that you will have to save the highlighted extract from the spreadsheet in an appropriate format, shut down the spreadsheet application and then retrieve the saved extract as a file into your word-processed document.

Your text should now include the data from the spreadsheet.

4. Adjusting the layout

Looking at her document, Judith decides that the layout of the table could be improved. She highlights the columns and then indents the highlighted block by 3 cm, using the PARAGRAPH option from the FORMAT menu.

As always, there are different ways of doing this. If the columns have been imported into your document as an image, it should be possible to click on the image and drag it to wherever you wish to place it.

5. Importing the graphs

Judith now needs to import the two graphs that she created within the spreadsheet (see Activity 7). She moves the cursor through the word-processed text to the place where she needs to insert the first chart and once again selects the NEW PAGE option from the INSERT menu.

She then selects INSERT from the toolbar and chooses the INSERT CHART. She is now shown the spreadsheet with a list of available chart displays. She chooses the bar chart she wants by clicking on the name 3D-GRAPH. The chart is automatically inserted into her document.

She does exactly the same with the line graph called LINE-GRAPH, making sure it is pasted into the correct place.

There are different ways of importing graphs from spreadsheets, eg:

● selecting the graph, copying it and pasting it into the document, as Judith did with the spreadsheet data;
● retrieving the file with the graph into your destination document.

Your text should now include the two graphs.

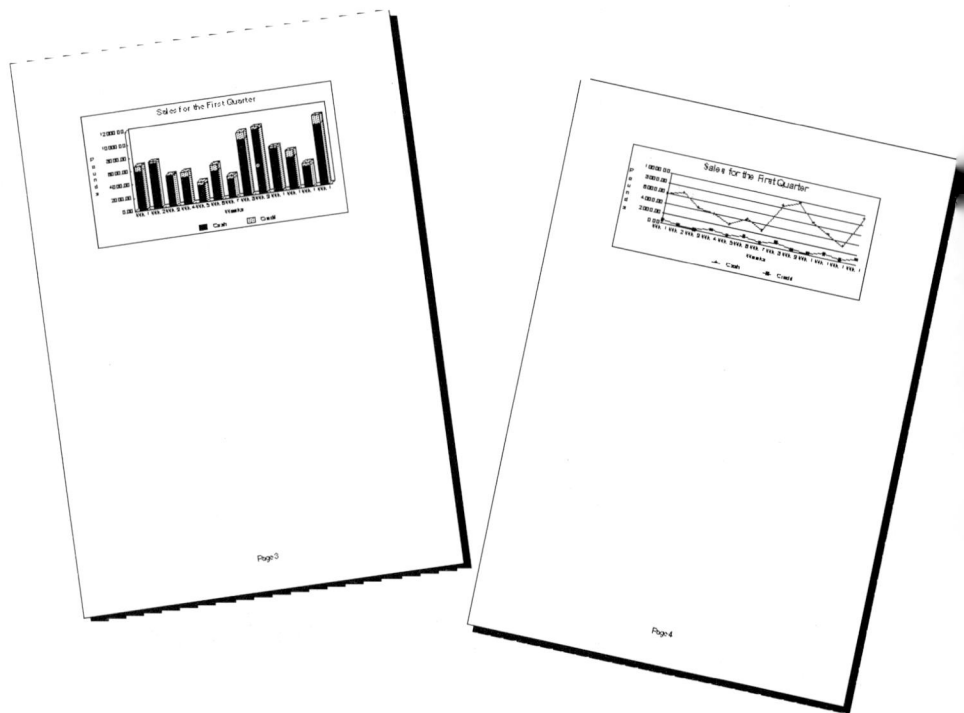

As the specification was that each diagram should be shown on a separate page, it is unlikely that the graphs will be split across pages.

6. Adjusting the display of the graphs

The graphs need to be fitted neatly across the report. Select each of them in turn and adjust the sizes so that they spread across most of the page width. When you select an image on screen, a box appears around it with eight sizing marks which you can click on and drag to resize the image.

Guidance

Unlike this report, the bulk of most reports consists of text. This will provide you with plenty of opportunity to customise and apply text styles (e.g. heading, sub-heading, normal), thus contributing to the LEVEL 3 requirement to 'create style sheets'.

7. Adjusting the text to the display

Once both the graphs are in place, Judith makes any adjustments to the text display that she thinks are necessary to improve the presentation of the report (e.g. typeface, bold, italics).

Look at your overall document and make improvements to the text display as you see fit.

8. Incorporating the Oasis information

Using similar techniques, Judith includes the spreadsheet showing the Oasis sales (refer to Activity 13). This is placed on a new page.

She then includes the publicity material produced by Gurdip (refer to Activity 4). This, too, is placed on its own page.

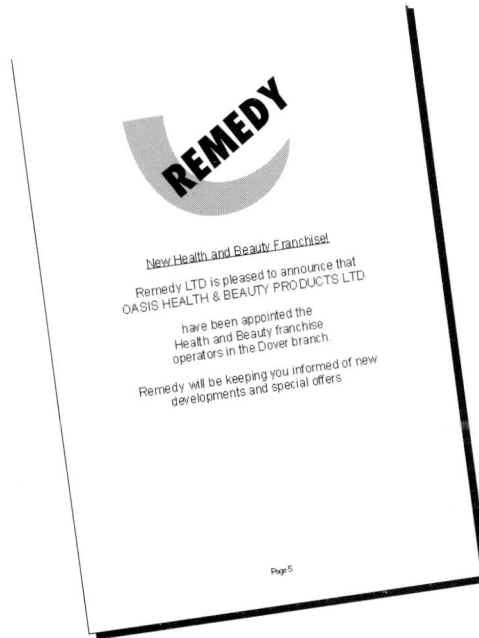

9. Numbering the pages

Guidance

It is often the case that front or cover pages are not included in numbering systems. For this reason, the second page might be numbered 1 and so on. Many programs provide a facility to turn off numbering on the first page.

The report now spreads over more than one page, so the pages need to be numbered. Judith decides to insert the numbers across the bottom of the pages. From the VIEW menu Judith chooses HEADERS & FOOTERS. In the footer box she types 'Page' followed by a space followed by '&p' which is the code for page numbers. Her software automatically centres the number.

Your program may insert page numbers in a different way. For instance, you may have a PAGE NUMBER option on an INSERT menu or on a FORMAT menu. Find out how to activate the page-numbering facility on your program and insert page numbers in your report.

10. Checking and previewing

Judith now previews how the report will look when printed out by choosing the PRINT PREVIEW option from the FILE menu. This is what it looks like.

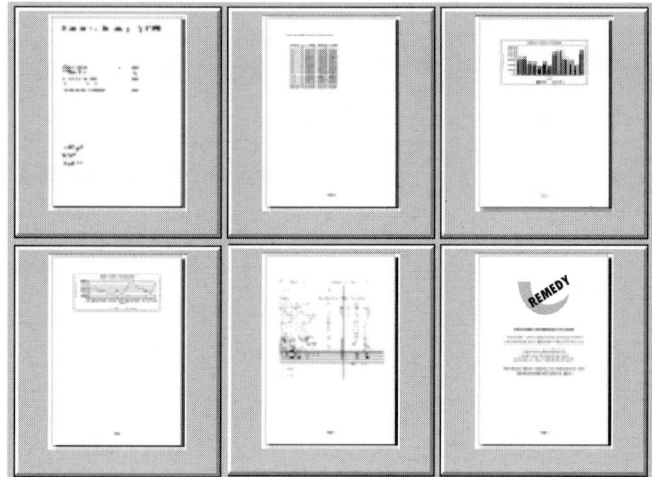

Your report should look similar!

11. Printing and saving

When she is satisfied with the layout and text of the report, Judith saves it and prints it out. She saves it with the name REPORT1.

Remember to save your document under an appropriate name before you close down the application.

EVIDENCE

Assignment 6 (page 93) provides an opportunity to produce evidence of compiling information and producing a report.

EVIDENCE OPPORTUNITIES

Gathering evidence of achievement

Evidence of achievement can be gathered from:

- previous education and experience;
- work carried out for any GNVQ or NVQ unit;
- work carried out on any other education programme (e.g. GCSE, A level, A/S level);
- experience outside education (e.g. in a part-time job, a hobby, a club, etc.).

Assignments and projects

In practice, when following a programme of study, you will carry out assignments and projects that cover a number of elements simultaneously.

The elements of Information Technology are inter-related:

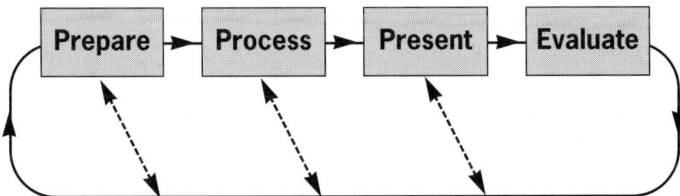

For the purpose of assessment, however, it may be necessary for you to break down what you have done, in order to show that you have satisfied the Performance Criteria and Range for the particular elements of Information Technology.

Cover all performance criteria

The evidence you provide must be meaningful. That is, you should have used IT *for a purpose*. Your evidence should not be bitty or just cover one performance criterion. For example, if you produce a document as evidence for *Element 2.1 or 3.1: Process Information*, you can't claim that you have reorganised information (PC 1) if you have not saved the document as you go along (PC 5). If the criteria are applicable to a particular activity, you must satisfy them all, and show evidence that you have done so.

Cover all parts of range

The range statements put the Performance Criteria into context and specify what you need to cover to fulfil them. For instance, in order to show that you can work with a variety of software applications, it is necessary to work with different types of information – text, graphics and numbers.

Record the type of information for each activity to ensure that you cover the range necessary. All range dimensions must be covered.

Presenting your evidence to an assessor

At the beginning of your programme of study you should make sure that you are clear about who will assess your work. Often you will be taught by a number of people, and it is the responsibility of those teaching you to make plain to you the arrangements for assessment. **If you are not clear, ask.**

The more well-organised you are in presenting evidence of achievement, the more you will help assessors to make reliable judgements about your work. This in turn will help you to learn and develop.

How to record achievement

Keep a portfolio to collect your evidence. You must also include an indication of which Performance Criteria and Range each piece of evidence has covered.

Whatever types of recording you use, it is essential to show how the *Performance Criteria* for the particular *level* you wish to achieve have been satisfied, together with the requirements of *Range* (e.g. that you have worked with the full range of types of information).

Here is a summary of the Evidence Indicators listed in the 1995 specifications to help you compile your portfolio of evidence.

What should go in your portfolio:

1) Samples of the source information selected.

2) Sample printouts of at least two examples each of text, graphics and numbers, before (i.e. what has been input) during and at the end of processing, with annotations to show how the information was input to make it easy to edit and to show the effects of using all the editing techniques in the range, reorganising information, and making calculations.

3) Printouts of information both before and after information has been combined from different sources. This should include printouts showing at least one example of importing information of the same type and at least one example of importing information of different types. The final printouts should show the combined information edited into the same format.

4) Backup copies of files and printouts of file directories showing how the files containing the information which has been input have been named to give an indication of their content and organised into directories.

5) Backup copies of files containing combined information.

6) An example of at least two different ways of presenting the same information, accompanied by an explanation of why one has been selected which best meets requirements.

7) An explanation and justification of the reasons for using information technology in relation to particular tasks. The explanation should cover both an account of why and how you have chosen to use information technology and the reasons for the use of information technology by others such as a commercial, industrial or public sector organisation. The explanation should include a comparison of the speed, ease of use, effort and accuracy of using information technology against using manual methods for preparing, processing and presenting the same information for the particular task, together with a description of software facilities used.

8) A short report evaluating at least three examples of systems for managing information comparing IT-based methods and non IT-based methods.

9) A log of errors and faults that occurred with the information technology used during the task with an evaluation of the effects of software faults, equipment faults and system faults on the user.

10) An explanation of working safely and in line with good working practices in relation to your use of information technology.

11) Records of observation by the assessor of you
   a making immediate corrections to errors noticed on entry
   b putting right any simple equipment faults which occur and regularly saving work
   c finding information
   d saving work before and after important changes

For level 3 only:

12) A printout of at least one example of a style sheet which you have set up.

13) A printout of at least one example of a spreadsheet template which you have set up.

14) A printout of at least one example of a database structure which you have set up.

15) A printout of at least one other example of an automated routine which you have set up.

If you follow the suggestions for evidence opportunities in this section you should fulfil most of the above Evidence Indicators. It may be that some of your pieces of evidence will be an amalgamation of two or more of them.

Suggestions for assignments

On the pages that follow your will find suggestions for assignments to improve your performance in Information Technology and to help you build your portfolio of evidence of achievement. These assignments may supplement those you will complete as part of your programme of study. The following list will help you choose the assignments that are appropriate for the level you wish to achieve.

		Level 2	Level 3
1	Keep a log of errors and faults	✓	✓
2	Preparing a cover sheet for your folder	✓	✓
3	Apply for a work placement	✓	✓
4	Prepare a poster	✓	✗
5	Record personal expenditure and income	✓	✓
6	Draw up a safety report	✓	✓
7	A stock control database	✓	✗
8	Sending a stock order to the supplier	✓	✓
9	Access on-line information	✗	✓
10	Modify a spreadsheet to show credit card charges	✗	✓
11	Evaluate ways of using Information Technology	✓	✓
12	Compile a folder of evidence	✗	✓
13	File management	✗	✓

1. Keep a log of errors and faults

Over the period of learning, practising and working through the Remedy Group *Practice Activities*, you are likely to come across a number of errors and faults while setting-up, inputting, manipulating and outputting information. These may include hardware, software and user faults.

Such faults have to be dealt with one way or another. You might be able to overcome the fault yourself or you may have to call for help. Sometimes you might bypass the fault, without putting it right.

Keep a record of the problems you encounter over as long a period as possible.

Suggested steps
1) Fill in the log sheet below, or use one of your own, as you encounter errors and problems.
2) Present the log sheet to your tutor, and discuss the implications.

Record of errors, problems and safety checks			
Type of problem	Date	Action taken	Supervisor initials

Candidate's signature ———————————
Assessor's signature ———————————

2. Prepare a cover sheet for your folder

In order to demonstrate your competence you will need to gather evidence and present it in a folder.

Create a drawing or a design which will be used as a cover sheet for your folder. The design does not have to be complicated, and you can ask others for help. However, you must show that you can actually use drawing facilities on a computer.

Suggested steps

1) Select appropriate line thicknesses.
2) Draw an appropriate image.
3) Create a border with a pattern.
4) Save the file on disk, using a suitable name.
5) The cover sheet needs a title. Give it one (for example, 'IT assignments').

6) Add your name to the cover sheet.
7) Improve the appearance of your text by changing size and font as appropriate.
8) Preview the draft, check and make any changes as appropriate.
9) Print the cover sheet.
10) Save the amended version of the file on disk, using a suitable name.

3. Apply for a work placement

You have decided to write a letter to a local firm, asking for a work placement. Here is an example of the sort of letter you might write:

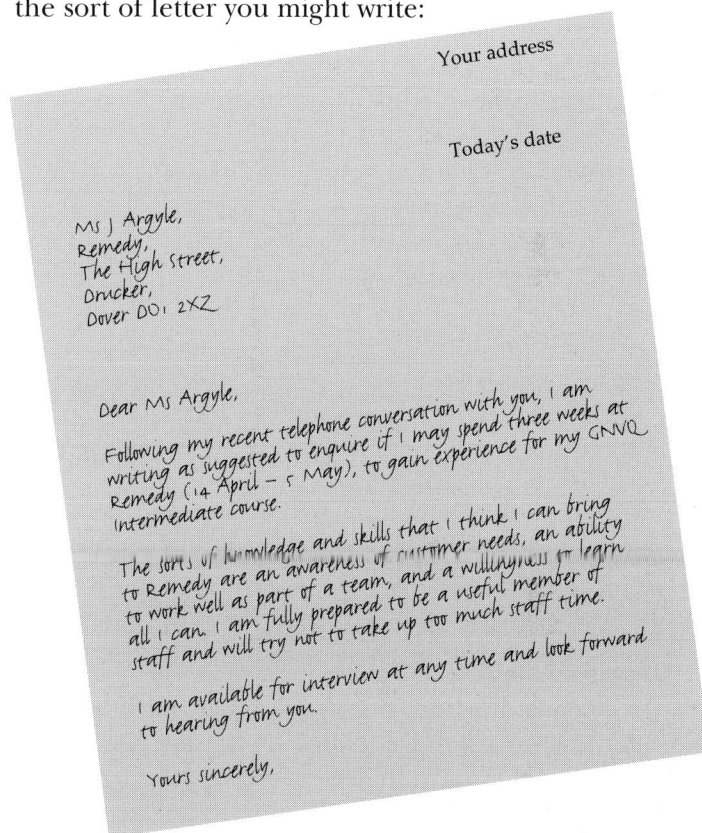

Your address

Today's date

Ms J Argyle,
Remedy,
The High Street,
Drucker,
Dover DO1 2XZ

Dear Ms Argyle,

Following my recent telephone conversation with you, I am writing as suggested to enquire if I may spend three weeks at Remedy (14 April – 5 May), to gain experience for my GNVQ Intermediate course.

The sorts of knowledge and skills that I think I can bring to Remedy are an awareness of customer needs, an ability to work well as part of a team, and a willingness to learn all I can. I am fully prepared to be a useful member of staff and will try not to take up too much staff time.

I am available for interview at any time and look forward to hearing from you.

Yours sincerely,

Suggested steps
1) Make some notes (on a scrap of paper) of the key points to be covered. (This is just to help you to identify key points and gather your thoughts. You can throw it away later.)
2) Select the software application to be used (for example, Word Processor, Desktop Publisher).
3) Set up the margins.
4) Enter your address at an appropriate place (for example, at the top right).
5) Enter the date, using today's date.
6) Enter the destination address.
7) Enter the salutation (for example, Dear Ms Argyle).

8) Key in appropriate text, left and right justified.
9) Enter your name at the end.
10) Check for errors and use the spell check facility.
11) Check the text against your notes and the example above to see whether you have covered the essential points.
12) Improve the text and layout as appropriate.
13) Print a draft copy of the letter.
14) NB: there are various conventions regarding ways of locating the addresses and displaying the layout – whatever you decide to adopt make sure you have been consistent. At this stage you might ask somebody else to see if they can make any suggestions for improvements.
15) Make changes, if required.
16) Preview the document and make any final changes.
17) Save the report on your own disk using a suitable filename.
18) Print two copies and sign your name.
19) File one copy and post the other.

4. Prepare a poster

Look at page 26 and draw up a poster for the general public which highlights the main feature of the photographic processing service offered by Photon.

Ensure that the poster has a border around the main frame. Inside this frame insert the heading and text, as appropriate. Select a text size and format which displays as much as possible on an A4 sheet.

Suggested steps
1) Make a directory on the disk (hard or floppy) using an appropriate directory name (for example, your initials).
2) Select the software application to be used and create a frame for an A4 page.
3) Place an attractive border on the edge of this frame.
4) Inside the frame insert the text NEW PHOTOGRAPHIC PROCESSING SERVICE and format it as a heading for the poster.
5) Make sure the heading occupies two lines, is centred and in a large typeface.
6) Key in the key points as highlighted on the letter shown on page 26.
7) Check it for errors.
8) Centre the text.
9) Enlarge all the text sufficiently in order for it to occupy most of the frame (i.e. minimising the gap at the bottom).

10) Print it out as a draft. Save the notice on your own disk using a suitable filename.
11) Change the presentation from portrait to landscape. Make any suitable adjustments and print out the copy. Save the notice on your own disk using another, suitable filename.
12) Decide which version is clearer and more appropriate.
13) Make a backup of the version you prefer, using a suitable backup filename. Write protect this file using an appropriate method. Delete the version that you are not using.

5. Record personal expenditure and income

In order to obtain a clear picture of the state of your individual finances, a picture of income and expenditure needs to be given.

Suggested steps
1) Plan out and note your daily expenses. This includes meals, college books, travel, clothes and sundry expenses such as cigarettes, drink, leisure activities, etc.
2) Enter your income for the week. This should include any allowances given to you and money received from part-time employment.
3) Enter all the details on a spreadsheet so that a complete picture is given.
4) Generate a TOTAL EXPENSES figure for the week
5) Generate a CASH LEFT OVER total for the week.
6) Display all numbers right justified.
7) Display all text in the left column left justified.
8) Display the costs and income in pounds and pence.
9) Check the spreadsheet data against your source notes and make any corrections.
10) Print the spreadsheet, making sure it all fits on one page.
11) Save your file on your own floppy disk.
12) Label your disk, using appropriate conventions such as your name, date and contents.
13) Print the modified spreadsheet structure.
14) Produce computer-generated graphs and charts which relate to your expenditure items.
15) Label the axes appropriately.
16) Evaluate the effectiveness (either verbally or in writing) of this use of a spreadsheet and associated facilities.

6. Draw up a safety report

Prepare a safety report on the location and the use of IT around you. Investigate the physical layout of IT equipment in a room where you use IT. Look out for the safety features as identified on pages 47–50. Your report should include:

A) your name and the date
B) numbered pages
C) a description of equipment and room layout
D) a section on cables and wiring
E) a section on light and reflection
F) a section on seating
G) a section on storage of magnetic media
H) a section on safety and warning signs
I) a conclusion, including, when appropriate, recommendations for action.

Suggested steps

1) Read pages 47–8 of this book and identify potential hazards, both to the safety of humans and the processing of information.
2) Prepare the report as specified above.
3) Check for errors and use a spell check.
4) Print a draft copy of the report.
6) Save the report on your own disk using a suitable filename.
5) Read the draft, correct the errors, and improve the layout as appropriate.
6) Save the report on your own disk with another suitable filename. Write protect this file, using an appropriate method.
7) Present both your draft and final version of your report to your tutor and discuss the implications.
8) LEVEL 3: create a style sheet for the document and apply paragraph styles as appropriate.

7. A stock control database

A stock record of the Oasis line of products has already been set up using a spreadsheet (see Activity 13). The manager of the Dover branch has also thought about using a database program to keep track of sales and the stock levels. This must show the order code, minimum number of each item required to be kept in stock, the number in stock, the number to be re-ordered, the retail price and the value of the items in stock. This last figure is to be generated automatically by the database.

Order code	Description	Min stock	In stock	Number to order	Shop price	Value of stock
AOBL	ALMOND OIL BODY LOTION	8	2	6	4	
ACB	AZTEC COLOUR BOX	2	1	1	14.99	
TCB	TAHITI COLOUR BOX	2	6	0	14.99	
ACB	ALPINE COLOUR BOX	2	4	0	14.99	
OJEC	OCEAN JEWELS EYE COLOURS	4	6	0	4.99	
FSEC	FOREST SECRETS EYE COLOURS	4	11	0	4.99	
DFEC	DESERT FLOWERS EYE COLOURS	4	0	4	4.99	
PLC	PAPRIKA LIP COLOURS	12	11	1	4.99	
CLC	CINNAMON LIP COLOURS	4	2	2	4.99	
JLC	JASMINE LIP COLOURS	8	2	6	4.99	
NKS	NATURAL KELP SHAMPOO	8	8	0	3.99	
NKC	NATURAL KELP CONDITIONER	8	6	2	2.99	
PFBL	PASSION FRUIT BODY LOTION	8	2	6	3.5	
AMFL	APPLE MINT FOOT LOTION	8	6	2	1.75	
CAM	CRUSHED APRICOT MOISTURISER	20	26	0	3.99	
BFWC	BANANA FACIAL WASH CREAM	8	14	0	1.9	
PDC	PAPAYA DEEP CLEANSER	20	14	6	2.1	
PSD	PINEAPPLE SCRUB DEFOLIANT	12	9	3	2.75	
LGAW	LEMON GRASS ASTRINGENT WASH	8	2	6	1.75	
WGST	WHITE GRAPE SKIN TONIC	8	0	8	1.5	

Suggested steps
1) Write down the name of the fields, their length, and the field types.
2) Ensure that you keep a record of the number of items, the code, the name, the description of units, the minimum number required and the number to be re-ordered.
3) Enter the data.
4) Check the details against the source documentation to see if they are accurate.
5) Sort and print the data.
6) Generate a report on items which require re-ordering. Save this report.
7) Save the file and close down.
8) Compare your use of the database with the use of the spreadsheet in Activity 13 and report your findings to your tutor.

8. Sending a stock order to the supplier

In the previous activity you found out which items require re-ordering from Oasis.

Now write a letter to them, generating the order, and include in this the appropriate extract from the report generated in the previous activity.

Suggested steps
1) Select the software application to be used (for example, Word Processor, Database).
2) Enter the text.
3) Combine this with the relevant parts of the database report, resolving differences of format.
4) Print the report and save it.
5) Present the report to your tutor and describe which facilities you used and the advantages and disadvantages of using the ones selected.

9. Access on-line information (for Level 3 only)

In order to obtain LEVEL 3 accreditation you need to show that you have communicated with other computers. It is important to remember that there is more to Information Technology than stand alone computers. Nowadays it is possible to access massive databases and powerful computers by using modems and networks. In order to obtain LEVEL 3 core skill accreditation you need to show how you have communicated with other computers.

You are not expected to be a technical genius. You do not have to configure settings etc. Use a system which has already been configured, for instance in an open learning centre or in a workplace. But you are expected to communicate with another system. You can send messages or you can obtain information. You can even download programs, as was described briefly in Activity 14 of this book.

Suggested steps
1) Obtain access to an on-line service.
2) Look up any information which is relevant to your workplace or your course.
3) Print out extracts.
4) Use this information as appropriate.

10. Modify a spreadsheet to show credit card charges (for Level 3 only)

In Activity 6 (pages 36–42) you had to create a spreadsheet which totalled Cash and Credit income for 13 weeks.

This does not take into account the fact that there is a charge on credit transactions. Assume that the cost of this is 2%. You will need to change the spreadsheet to take this into account.

The next step will be to find out the effect of passing the charge on to the customer. Set up a cell which contains the reference for the credit mark up, and adjust the credit incomes according to the mark up you are thinking of charging. (You should use absolute referencing when referring to the cell with the charge rates.)

Suggested steps
1) Select or set up the spreadsheet as shown in Activity 6.
2) Set up, on a new row, either near the top or below the main table, a cell for the credit charges and label the cell appropriately.
3) Insert a new column to show the adjustments in income and, using an absolute reference, generate the amended total for Week 1.
4) Replicate these totals for the remaining weeks.
5) Add another column which shows how much you will need to charge the customer in order to recoup the charges from the credit card companies.
6) Add the date and a title to the spreadsheet display.
7) Print out three reports, showing charges of 0%, 1% and 2%.
8) Save the spreadsheet, using another name, indicating the version number.

11. Evaluate ways of using Information Technology

Describe and evaluate the use of IT on your course or in your workplace. This is best done *after* you have done most of the other assignments.

Explain:

A) Why accuracy and precision are important (for example, when inputting data and printing out reports).

B) What should be done to help to prevent losing data through accidents (for example, by deleting the wrong files)?

C) What routines can be used to secure information (for example, passwords, file access labels)?

D) What should be done to help to prevent losing data (for example, a computer crash)?

E) What should be done to help to prevent unauthorised people from gaining access to confidential data?

F) How might IT be used to save time, reduce costs, increase efficiency and improve accuracy?

G) In what ways do the applications which handle text (for example, a word processing program), graphics (for example, a graphics package) and numbers (for example, a payroll program or a spreadsheet) affect and improve the efficiency of day-to-day working?

H) How the things that you have done with Information Technology could also have been done in other ways?

I) The effects of Information Technology problems upon users.

J) LEVEL 3: how using IT might not be the best solution.

K) LEVEL 3: how systems used by others for preparing, processing and presenting information compare with those you have used.

Suggested steps

1) Use a word-processing or desktop publishing program to prepare notes on each of the above items, drawing upon your experiences when appropriate.
2) Print and save your notes.
3) Present your notes to your tutor.
4) Discuss your findings.

12. Compile a folder of evidence

In order to demonstrate your competence you will need to gather your pieces of evidence and present them in a folder. One of the requirements for LEVEL 2 and LEVEL 3 information technology core skills is that different forms of information are combined. This can be demonstrated by compiling your different pieces of evidence and presenting them as one or a combined document. (This should only be done where appropriate.) Presentation is important.

Prepare a report, which must be word processed or desktop published.

Suggested steps

1) Decide which items can be combined.
2) Decide which are to be referenced as an appendix.
3) The report should include:

A) a front cover with a title, your name, the date
B) numbered pages
C) date stamping (LEVEL 3 only)
D) an index (LEVEL 3 only)
E) create style sheets for text and apply the styles as appropriate (LEVEL 3 only)

4) Print, save and backup the report.

13. Back up files and file management

Organise all your saved work in a sensible way and make back up copies of all your files.

Suggested steps

1) Examine all the files you have used and created while working through the practice activities and assessment opportunities.
2) Decide how they can be sorted. It may make sense (for classification purposes and due to quantity) to put different types of data on separate disks. Identify sub-directories to be used.
3) Format one or more floppy disks as appropriate.
4) Label the disk(s).
5) Write an appropriate name and the date on the label.
6) Create directories as appropriate.
7) Copy the source files into the appropriate directories.
8) Write protect the disk(s).
9) Keep the disk(s) in a safe place.

IT Core Skills

IT — PREPARE INFORMATION

Level 2	Level 3	Element	Detail	Log of faults & errors	Preparing a cover sheet	Letter	Preparing a poster	Personal expenditure	Draw up a safety report	Stock control	Stock order	On-line information	Modify a spreadsheet	Evaluating the use of IT	Compiling a folder of evidence	File management
2.1.1	3.1.1	select information appropriate to the task		–	Y	Y	Y	Y	Y	Y	Y	–	Y	Y	Y	–
		select	information taken from existing sources	–	–	P	Y	P	Y	Y	Y	–	P	–	Y	–
			information developed during input	–	Y	Y	–	P	Y	–	Y	–	P	Y	–	–
		information	text	–	Y	Y	Y	Y	Y	Y	Y	–	Y	Y	Y	–
			graphics	–	Y	–	P	–	–	–	–	–	–	–	Y	–
			numbers	–	–	–	–	Y	–	Y	Y	–	Y	–	Y	–
2.1.2	3.1.2	enter information into software in ways that will make it easy to edit		–	Y	Y	Y	Y	Y	Y	Y	–	–	Y	Y	–
		enter	inputting source information accurately	–	–	Y	Y	Y	Y	Y	Y	–	–	Y	–	–
			making immediate corrections to errors noticed on entry	–	–	Y	P	Y	Y	Y	P	–	–	Y	–	–
			putting right simple equipment faults	Y	P	P	P	P	P	P	P	P	P	P	P	P
			using manuals and on-line help facilities	Y	P	P	P	P	P	P	P	P	P	P	P	P
			asking for help as appropriate	Y	P	P	P	P	P	P	P	P	P	P	P	P
		information	text	–	Y	Y	Y	Y	Y	Y	Y	–	Y	Y	Y	–
			graphics	–	Y	–	P	–	–	–	–	–	–	–	Y	–
			numbers	–	–	–	–	Y	–	Y	Y	–	Y	–	Y	–
		software	for text	–	P	Y	Y	–	Y	Y	Y	–	–	Y	Y	–
			for graphics	–	Y	–	–	–	–	–	–	–	–	–	P	–
			for numbers	–	–	–	–	Y	–	Y	–	–	Y	–	P	–
2.1.3.	3.1.3	keep source information required for task		–	–	–	–	Y	–	Y	–	–	–	Y	–	–
2.1.4	3.1.4	store input systematically and make backup copies		–	P	P	Y	P	Y	–	–	–	Y	–	Y	Y
		store input systematically	naming files sensibly to indicate the contents	–	Y	Y	–	Y	Y	P	–	–	–	P	Y	Y
			locating files conveniently for subsequent use	–	–	–	–	Y	Y	P	–	–	–	P	Y	Y
			creating and using directories to group related files	–	–	–	–	–	–	–	–	–	–	–	P	Y
			saving work before and after important changes	–	Y	–	Y	Y	Y	–	–	–	–	P	–	–
			saving work when all the information has been input	–	Y	Y	Y	Y	Y	Y	–	–	–	Y	Y	–
	3.1 5	configure software to aid input of information		–	–	–	–	Y	Y	Y	–	–	–	Y	Y	–
		software	creating style sheets for text	–	–	–	–	–	Y	–	–	–	–	–	Y	–
			creating spreadsheet templates for numbers	–	–	–	–	Y	–	–	–	–	Y	–	Y	–
			creating database structures	–	–	–	–	–	–	Y	–	–	–	–	–	–

IT — PROCESS INFORMATION

Level 2	Level 3	Element	Detail	Log of faults & errors	Preparing a cover sheet	Letter	Preparing a poster	Personal expenditure	Draw up a safety report	Stock control	Stock order	On-line information	Modify a spreadsheet	Evaluating the use of IT	Compiling a folder of evidence	File management
2.2.1	3.2.1	find information required for the task –		–	–	–	–	–	–	–	–	Y	Y	P	–	Y
		find	by looking in the right directory	–	–	–	–	–	–	–	–	P	P	P	–	Y
			by looking for files with a given name	–	–	–	–	–	–	–	–	Y	–	P	–	Y
			by searching for information which meets specified requirements	–	–	–	–	–	–	–	–	Y	Y	–	–	Y
			by accessing remote sources	–	–	–	–	–	–	–	–	Y	–	–	–	–
2.2.2	3.2.2	use appropriate software to edit information		–	P	P	P	Y	Y	Y	Y	Y	P	P	Y	–
		software	for text	–	P	Y	Y	Y	Y	Y	Y	–	–	Y	Y	–
			for graphics	–	Y	–	P	–	–	–	–	–	–	–	P	–
			for numbers	–	–	–	–	Y	–	Y	–	–	Y	–	P	–
		edit	amending	–	P	P	Y	P	P	P	P	–	Y	P	Y	–
			moving	–	–	P	P	P	P	P	P	–	–	P	Y	–
			reformatting	–	Y	Y	Y	Y	Y	Y	P	–	–	P	Y	–
			copying	–	–	P	P	P	P	P	P	–	Y	P	Y	–
			deleting	–	–	P	P	P	P	P	P	–	P	P	P	–
			inserting	–	Y	P	P	P	P	P	P	–	P	P	Y	–
		information	text	–	Y	Y	Y	–	Y	Y	Y	–	–	Y	Y	–
			graphics	–	Y	–	–	–	–	–	–	–	–	–	P	–
			numbers	–	–	–	–	Y	–	Y	Y	–	Y	–	P	–
2.2.3	3.2.3	process numerical information by using software to make calculations		–	–	–	–	Y	–	Y	–	–	Y	–	–	–
		make calculations	by creating totals in databases and spreadsheets	–	–	–	–	Y	–	Y	–	–	Y	–	–	–
			by using formulas incorporating absolute and relative references to spreadsheet cells	–	–	–	–	–	–	–	–	–	Y	–	–	–
2.2.4	3.2.4	reorganise information as required for the task		–	–	–	–	–	Y	Y	Y	–	Y	P	Y	Y
		reorganise	sorting	–	–	–	–	–	–	Y	–	–	–	–	P	P
			restructuring stored information	–	–	–	–	Y	–	Y	–	–	Y	P	Y	–
2.2.5	3.2.5	save work at appropriate intervals –		–	Y	Y	–	–	Y	Y	–	P	–	Y	Y	–
		appropriate intervals	before and after important changes	–	Y	–	–	–	Y	P	–	–	–	–	–	–
			when the processing is complete	–	Y	Y	Y	–	Y	Y	Y	–	–	Y	Y	–
2.2.6	3.2.6	combine information from different sources, resolving differences of format		–	–	–	–	–	–	–	–	Y	–	–	Y	–
		combine	importing information of the same type	–	–	–	–	–	–	–	–	Y	–	–	Y	–
			importing information of a different type	–	P	–	–	–	–	–	–	Y	–	–	Y	–
	3.2.7	create automated routines that aid efficient processing of information		–	–	–	–	–	–	Y	–	–	Y	–	Y	–

Y = yes   P = possible

IT Core Skills

Column headers (left to right): Log of faults & errors · Preparing a cover sheet · Letter · Preparing a poster · Personal expenditure · Draw up a safety report · Stock control · Stock order · On-line information · Modify a spreadsheet · Evaluating the use of IT · Compiling a folder of evidence · File management

IT — PRESENT INFORMATION

Level 2	Level 3	Description	Faults log	Cover sheet	Letter	Poster	Pers. expend.	Safety report	Stock control	Stock order	On-line info	Spreadsheet	Evaluating IT	Folder of evidence	File mgmt
	3.3.1	prepare information for presentation	–	–	–	–	–	Y	–	Y	–	Y	Y	Y	–
		prepare — selecting the form and content of the information to match the requirements of the task	–	–	–	–	–	Y	–	Y	–	Y	Y	–	–
		date-stamping and pagination of documents	–	–	–	–	–	Y	–	–	–	–	P	–	–
		using named directories for associated display files	–	–	–	–	–	–	–	–	–	–	–	–	–
		storing successive developments of information for presentation with version numbers and informative file names	–	–	–	–	–	Y	–	–	–	Y	–	–	–
2.3.1	3.3.2	present information in different ways & select which way best meets requirements of the task	–	P	–	Y	Y	–	Y	Y	–	Y	P	Y	–
		information — text	–	P	Y	Y	Y	Y	Y	Y	–	–	Y	Y	–
		graphics	–	Y	–	P	Y	–	–	–	–	–	–	Y	–
		numbers	–	–	–	Y	–	Y	Y	–	Y	–	Y	–	–
		requirements — fitness for purpose	–	P	Y	Y	Y	Y	–	Y	–	Y	Y	Y	–
		matched to audience	–	P	Y	Y	–	Y	–	Y	–	–	Y	Y	–
		clarity	–	Y	Y	Y	–	Y	Y	–	–	Y	Y	Y	–
		accuracy	–	Y	Y	Y	Y	Y	Y	–	–	Y	–	Y	–
		appropriate use of information referencing	–	–	–	–	–	Y	–	–	–	Y	–	Y	–
2.3.2	3.3.3	use appropriate software to display information	–	Y	–	Y	–	–	–	–	Y	–	–	Y	–
2.3.3	3.3.4	use appropriate software to produce hard copy of information	–	Y	Y	Y	Y	Y	Y	Y	–	Y	Y	Y	–
		software — for text	–	P	Y	Y	–	Y	Y	Y	–	–	–	Y	–
		for graphics	–	Y	–	P	–	–	–	–	–	–	–	Y	–
		for numbers	–	–	–	–	–	Y	Y	–	Y	–	–	–	–
2.3.4	3.3.5	present combined information in a consistent format	–	P	–	–	–	–	–	–	–	Y	–	Y	–
2.3.5	3.3.6	store information in files and make backup copies	–	P	P	Y	P	Y	–	–	–	Y	–	Y	Y

IT — EVALUATE THE USE OF IT

Level 2	Level 3	Description	Faults log	Cover sheet	Letter	Poster	Pers. expend.	Safety report	Stock control	Stock order	On-line info	Spreadsheet	Evaluating IT	Folder of evidence	File mgmt
2.4.1		explain the reasons for using information technology	–	–	–	–	–	–	–	–	–	Y	–	Y	–
	3.4.1	explain and justify the reasons for using information technology	–	–	–	–	–	–	–	–	–	Y	Y	Y	–
2.4.2		compare methods used by student for preparing, processing & presenting info	–	–	–	–	Y	–	Y	–	–	–	–	Y	–
	3.4.2	compare methods used by student and others for preparing, processing & presenting info	–	–	–	–	P	–	–	–	–	–	–	Y	–
		compare in terms of — speed	–	–	–	P	–	P	–	–	–	–	–	Y	–
		ease of use	–	–	–	–	–	–	–	–	–	P	–	Y	–
		effort	–	–	–	–	–	–	–	–	–	P	–	Y	–
		accuracy	–	–	–	–	–	–	–	–	–	P	–	Y	–
		methods — manual	–	–	–	–	–	–	–	–	–	–	–	Y	–
		alternative ways of using information technology	–	–	–	–	–	–	–	–	–	Y	–	Y	–
2.4.3	3.4.4	describe the software facilities used to meet the requirements of the task	–	–	–	–	–	–	–	–	–	Y	Y	Y	–
	3.4.3	evaluate alternative systems for managing information	–	–	–	–	–	–	–	–	–	Y	–	Y	–
		evaluate — effectiveness	–	–	–	–	Y	P	Y	–	–	–	–	Y	–
		cost	–	–	–	–	P	–	–	–	–	–	–	Y	–
		effects on employment	–	–	–	–	P	–	–	–	–	–	–	Y	–
		benefits to individuals	–	–	–	–	–	–	–	–	–	–	–	Y	–
		benefits to organisations	–	–	–	–	–	–	–	–	–	–	–	Y	–
		disadvantages to individuals	–	–	–	–	P	–	–	–	–	–	–	Y	–
		disadvantages to organisations	–	–	–	–	P	–	–	–	–	–	–	Y	–
		systems — manual	–	–	–	–	–	–	–	–	–	–	–	Y	–
		information technology	–	–	–	–	–	–	–	–	–	Y	–	Y	–
2.4.4	3.4.4	explain the effects on users of problems that can occur when using IT	–	Y	–	–	–	–	–	–	–	–	–	Y	–
		problems — errors	–	P	–	–	–	–	–	–	–	–	–	Y	–
		equipment faults	–	P	–	–	–	–	–	–	–	–	–	Y	–
		loss of information	–	P	–	–	P	–	–	–	–	–	–	Y	–
		system faults	–	P	–	–	P	–	–	–	–	–	–	Y	–
2.4.5	3.4.5	explain the importance of working safely & in line with good working practices	–	P	–	–	–	Y	–	–	–	–	–	P	–
		working safely — safety of the user	–	P	–	–	–	Y	–	–	–	–	–	P	–
		safety of the equipment	–	P	–	–	–	Y	–	–	–	–	–	P	–
		safety of the information	–	P	–	–	–	Y	–	–	–	–	–	P	–

Y = yes   P = possible

Databases

What is a database?

A database is a central data storage system in which information can be stored and easily retrieved. For example, a database might be used by a library to keep a computerised record of all its library books or by a shop to keep a computerised list of customers showing their credit ratings and the products they have bought.

In a manual card index system information is stored on filing cards. A filing card, from a system used for storing names and addresses, is shown below.

```
Penny Wilton
9 Upperdale Rd
Derby DE3 6AL
01332-345712
```

Figure 1

This card is known as a 'record'. On a computerised database, a record can contain exactly the same information, but, in order to store and retrieve the data properly, the structure needs to be more detailed and systematic.

Figure 1 shows one record from a database (the equivalent of one filing card). The record is divided into separate categories, known as 'fields'. Each field is given a name (listed down the left-hand side) and has a space in which to input the data. For example, in the field 'surname' the data 'Wilton' can be entered.

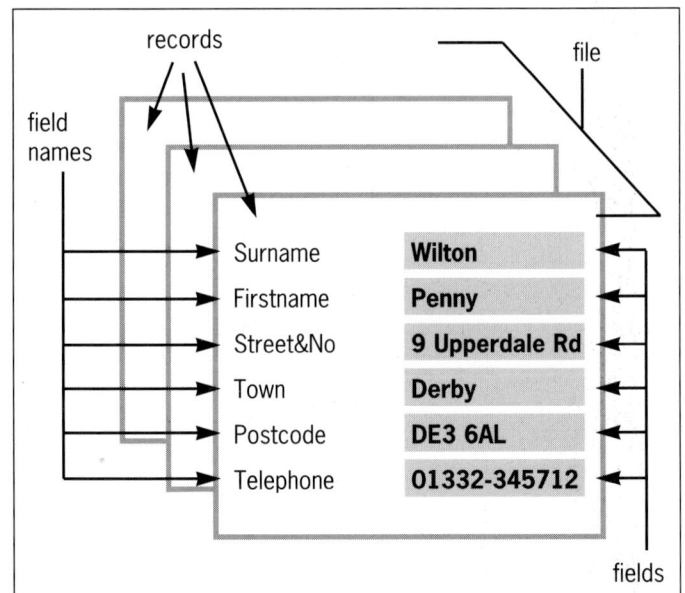

The collection of these records is usually called a 'datafile'. Sometimes a datafile will be called a database but, in practice, a database may contain a number of datafiles. Databases can hold enormous amounts of information. A key feature is that although you only need to input data once, that data can be used in many different ways.

Confusingly, the word 'database' is sometimes used to refer to a package, such as *dBase IV, DataEase, Foxpro, Access* or *Paradox*, which provides a structure for the storage of information. Such packages are more properly known as database management systems, or DBMS s.

The skills needed to maintain and use a database are the same whatever your purpose for using it – keeping an up-to-date address list, investigating historical records, keeping track of sales transactions, organising a stock-control system, or performing any similar data-orientated tasks.

Searching for information

You could find information on a database by looking through each of the records, one at a time, but this would be a slow process. One of the main reasons for using a database program is that its search facilities can find data quickly and efficiently. This is done by typing a word or code in a specified field (e.g. a surname you are looking for) and telling the program to retrieve all the records which contain that word or code in that field. For example, entering **Smith** in the surname field will result in all the records containing **Smith** in this field being found, regardless of the data in the other fields.

Some fields will always contain data that is unique to a record (e.g. invoice number, employee reference number, account number). These are called key fields. A specific record can be located directly if a key field is used as the search field.

Complex searches and logical operators

There are many ways of searching for information on a database. One way is to establish a series of conditions in order to narrow the search. For

Using a database programme will make searching for information quicker and more efficient...

instance, if you needed to find the address for someone called Joan Smith, you could enter **Joan** as the search criteria in the firstname field and the program would retrieve all records containing this name. However, if you entered **Joan** in the firstname field and **Smith** in the surname field, fewer records would be found as the program would only retrieve records with both Joan and Smith, and the particular record you are searching for would be located more quickly. This type of search can be expressed as a logical condition; it uses what is known as a logical AND. Both surname AND firstname are defined.

Another logical condition is OR. You might search for people who live in one postal code area, OR an adjacent one. A list of logical conditions (sometimes called operators) is given below:

Complex searches can usually be expressed in more

Logical Conditions	
Symbol	**Meaning**
=	equal to
>	greater than
<	less than
<>	not equal to
<=	less than or equal to
>=	greater than or equal to
AND	both conditions are met
OR	one condition is met
NOT	condition not met

Table 1

than one way. On certain databases these logical conditions can be incorporated in what is known as a query language. The following is an example of a query language in a search for members who have a driving licence AND who live either in Kent OR Surrey.

> for members
>
> with licence = 'Yes' AND county = 'Kent' OR county = 'Surrey'
>
> list records

Sorting information

Sorting is the process by which the program will put data into a required order that you have specified.

This is carried out by choosing the sort option from the menu and

- specifying the fields you want to sort

- specifying whether you require those fields (alphabetical or numerical) to appear in an ascending (A–Z or 1 …) or descending (Z–A or … 1) order.

Reporting

It is often necessary to present information from a database in a report, and there are various ways of doing this. The information may be printed, sent to disk, or displayed on the screen. The requirement to print out hard copy is most common.

The simplest report is one that shows one whole record. This is called 'form reporting'. However, you can also create reports which only show information from specified fields, presented in a table format.

For most purposes 'table reports' are far more effective because the information is displayed in a clear format suitable for quick reference. Tables also take up less paper (or fewer screens) than form reports. Database programs will generate a default table layout. Some of the more sophisticated programs allow you to customise tables, for example by altering headings, column widths, or the order of the fields, and by enabling the insertion of additional information such as the current date and a title for the report

Errors in data input can have far-reaching consequences....

There are many other ways of displaying and reporting data. For example, reporting facilities are often used to generate labels and standard letters.

Entering data

There are various things to remember when entering data:

- Ensure you have authorisation to enter data (your access to a complex database may be restricted).

- Identify any incomplete or incorrect source data.

- Check for any errors in your data entry (compare against source data).

- Bear in mind the fact that fields might be designed in such a way that only certain data can

Figure 2　A customised report

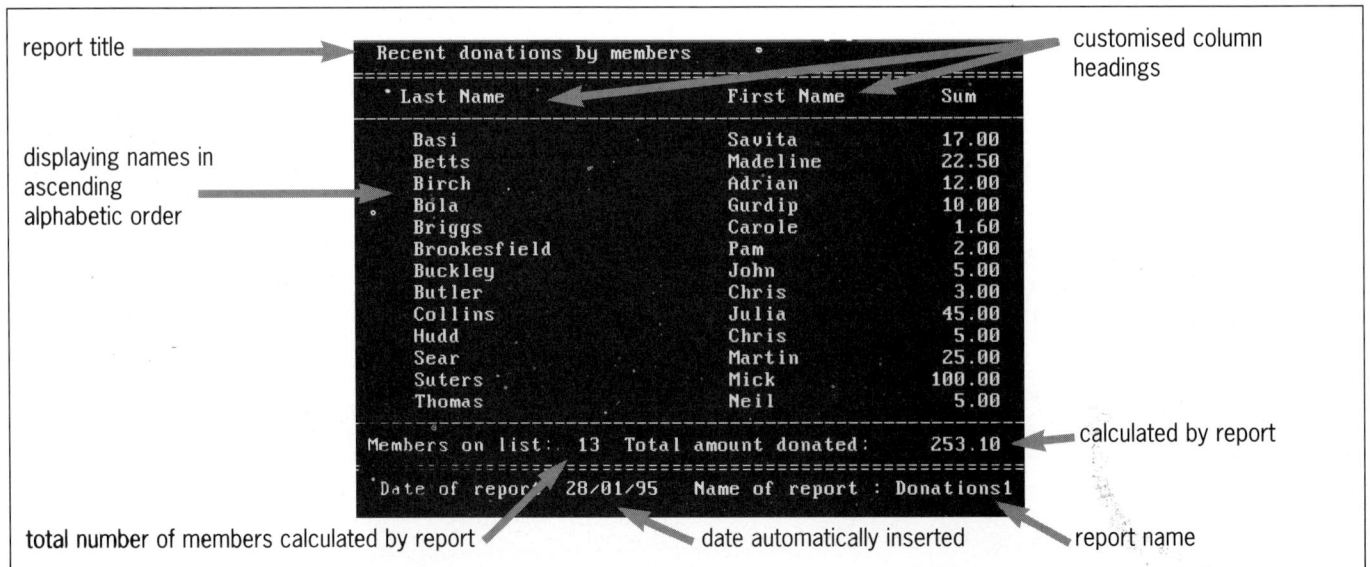

report title

customised column headings

Recent donations by members		
Last Name	First Name	Sum
Basi	Savita	17.00
Betts	Madeline	22.50
Birch	Adrian	12.00
Bola	Gurdip	10.00
Briggs	Carole	1.60
Brookesfield	Pam	2.00
Buckley	John	5.00
Butler	Chris	3.00
Collins	Julia	45.00
Hudd	Chris	5.00
Sear	Martin	25.00
Suters	Mick	100.00
Thomas	Neil	5.00

Members on list:　13　Total amount donated:　253.10

Date of report　28/01/95　Name of report : Donations1

displaying names in ascending alphabetic order

calculated by report

total number of members calculated by report

date automatically inserted

report name

be entered. For example – some fields may only accept numbers from a particular range or a word from a pre-defined list (created by whoever setup the database). There is almost always a length limitation to a field entry.

The data entry form

Databases usually have a special screen which is for the entry of data; this is commonly called a 'data entry form'. You can design the entry form to suit your purpose, including the order of entry, choice of colours and helpful screen messages.

Designing a record

There are different ways of designing a record, depending upon the program you are using. However, it is usual for the design to be done at the same time as setting up the data entry form. Before setting up the entry form, you should look at the source data and jot down the *name* of each field, the *length* of each field and the *type* of field you require.

You will then need to select the appropriate option from the menu (e.g. NEW FORM) and enter a name for your collection of records (a file). Any valid filename can be used but it is best if it reflects the information included. You should see a blank screen, or a default data entry form. It is now necessary to determine

- field locations
- field names
- field lengths
- field types

Field names

Most databases require names (sometimes known as field titles) to be given to every field. The field name is not to be confused with the content. Thus a field called 'surname' will contain different surnames (e.g. Wilton, Smith, Bola).

It is good practice not to use spaces or punctuation in field names and to keep them short and succinct. Avoid creating fields for which there is no specific need.

Field length

The length of each field is determined by two considerations. First, you have to decide what is the longest piece of data that is going to be put in that field. For example, the field for handling surnames will need to be long enough to take the longest surname which needs to be entered. Do not make the fields unnecessarily long – it will waste space, slow things down and can be a nuisance when it comes to presenting reports. The second reason for considering the length is that it may affect the speed of processing and the amount of memory available.

Field types

The main types of fields are

Numeric: This includes any number that might be used in calculations. Information stored in numeric fields will allow you to produce lists ordered by number.

Alphanumeric: This refers to letters of the alphabet and/or numbers (but the numbers are for reference only – such as telephone numbers – and cannot be used in calculations). Information stored in alphanumeric fields will allow you to produce alphabetical lists.

Date: This consists of any date.

Choice: This is a field in which only a choice from a pre-determined list can be entered. This standardises the entries and makes it easier to locate specific records at a later date. If the data entered does not appear in the pre-determined list it will not be accepted into the field. Thus, for example, fields set to MALE or FEMALE would not accept the entry MAN.

Your database program may enable you to specify the use of codes in place of a whole data item. For example, in a field that requires MALE or FEMALE you may wish to use the codes M and F. One way of doing this is by choosing a choice field, but there are other ways. An advantage of using codes is that they take up less memory in the database. The reduced amount of data to be entered also means mistakes are less likely to be made. However, codes should only be set up if there will be a sufficient number of data items to warrant them.

Powerful databases will allow you to set up

mandatory fields – in which information must be entered before the user can go any further. They will also allow you to create fields where the data is derived from other fields. The purpose might be to perform a calculation (e.g. addition of VAT, conversion of date of birth into age) or to create a unique identifier such as a reference number which includes the initials of the person's name.

The design of the structure, including display, of the file varies considerably between packages. The terms used also vary. The data entry form is called a 'form' in *DataEase* and *dBase*, and a 'folder' in *Access*. Sometimes a file is referred to as a 'database'.

Designing database applications

It is unlikely that you will be required to design massive databases. The design of these applications can be very complicated; you can't just dive in and learn as you go. Most database applications consist of a series of inter-related files and are called relational databases. Often data in one file is derived from another file. The designer will need to see how the separate files relate to each other and will need to define the relationships between them. In a library system, for example, a database might have one file for borrowers, another for loans, another for books, another for suppliers, and so on.

Sophisticated packages will store data in tables; but these may be hidden from the user.

There are no golden rules when designing databases; so much will depend upon the need and the program being used. Nevertheless, when designing a database, it is useful to remember :

- Each file should contain data relating to just one subject (or a main purpose). You would never, for example, place details of customers and products in the same file.

- Usually it is better not to split files into smaller files in the belief that they will be easier to manage. For example, in a filing cabinet staff may be divided into categories and filed separately, but on a database it is far better to put all the staff in the same file and create fields for the various categories.

In the database checklist below, fill in the keystrokes that you need to do in order to use the facilities listed down the left-hand side. This will help you to remember them.

Personal DATABASE checklist

Facility	Keystrokes
Copy data	_____
Create a report	_____
Delete a record	_____
Delete data in a field	_____
Edit data	_____
Enter data	_____
Exit program	_____
Find (or search)	_____
Go to the last record	_____
Go to the first record	_____
Help facility	_____
Insert/overwrite	_____
Insert a field	_____
Load a report	_____
Load program	_____
Logical AND	_____
Logical NOT	_____
Logical OR	_____
Modify record structure	_____
Next record	_____
Previous record	_____
Print report	_____
Printer type (or codes)	_____
Save data (or record or file)	_____
Set up file (design a record/form)	_____
Undo	_____

Desktop publishing

Use a scanner to incorporate images to enliven your documents.

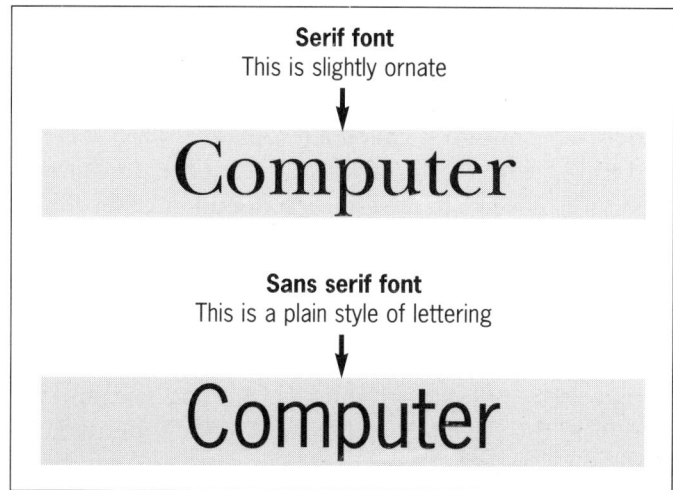

Figure 3

People use desktop publishing (DTP) packages to prepare high-quality documents which may contain graphics, different styles of text and a variety of fonts. (A font is a kind of typeface.) DTP packages were developed as a response to the limitations of word-processing programs. They contain the WYSIWYG facility (What You See Is What You Get) which means that the way the document appears on the screen is the same as it appears when it is printed out. DTP also offered many more fonts than any word-processing program, allowed blocks of text to be manipulated, and had facilities to create and use graphics.

Many of the facilities of desktop publishing packages are now included in word-processing programs. Consequently, the term 'desktop publishing' is used very loosely. Often when someone requires a desktop-published document, what they want is simply a document which looks professional and is produced on a high quality printer. But it is still the case that DTP packages, in comparison with word-processing programs, usually provide a greater degree of control over how a page is arranged, from the overall layout right down to the smallest detail.

Fonts

In a desktop publishing package there are generally a large number of fonts available. Most fonts fall into two families: serif and sans serif (see Figure 3).

It is possible to vary the size of a font without affecting the shape of the characters. The size is measured in points.

Points are units of measurement for typefaces. There are approximately 72 to the inch. The number of points refers to the height of each letter, but when the point size is changed the width of each letter automatically changes to remain balanced with the height. Most text in books or documents is normally set at between 9 and 12 points (this text is 10 pt).

10 Point

18 Point

24 Point

The higher the point the larger the size of the text.

Images

Desktop publishing documents can include photographs, drawings and graphs. These can be 'imported' into DTP documents from other computer packages. Once imported, they can be moved around, cut down or altered in size. Images can be inputted into the computer using a scanner which scans them, and produces a digitised image.

Consistency in styles

Most organisations like the style of their correspondence, reports and any published material to be consistent as this strengthens their corporate image. A basic design can be created for documents such as letters, reports and memorandums, which provides a framework into which text and data can be added. This design is called a template or style sheet and can be saved and retrieved at any time. In this way it is not necessary to design each document every time, saving time and effort. Large organisations often employ professional graphics artists to produce templates for them. (see Templates p. 119)

As part of your templates, it is also possible to specify certain styles of text including its font and size, and its layout on the page, e.g. centred, first line indented, aligned to the left. These styles are saved and can be called up and applied to any section of text, heading, sub-heading or other part of a document.

Another feature which can be changed and saved as a style of text is the space between the lines of text. This is known as the 'leading'. (The name leading is derived from the practice in the print industry of placing strips of lead between the lines of type.) The size of the leading is typically around 20% of the vertical height of the letters.

Design considerations

There are no golden rules when designing documents; so much depends upon the type of document you are producing and the program you are using. Although a beginner can produce simple documents using DTP, it takes someone of considerable expertise to use it to its full potential.

When designing a document or a template, it is useful to:

- look at existing designs

- remember who the intended reader is

- remember what the document is meant to achieve

- consider the limitations of the available printer (very precise specifications can only be dealt with effectively on a laser printer and many printers can only accept certain sizes of paper)

- take into account the potential return from the effort expended (it is often the case that a simple text document would suffice)

- only use a feature if it is useful

- keep the design simple

- be consistent (don't pick and mix styles)

- try using pencil and paper to draft out possible layouts

- make sure the template is completed before inputting any data

- use appropriate sizes and styles for your headings

- think about how to use 'white' space (empty spaces can be used to good effect; they are not simply left-over gaps)

- build your display around pictures (don't use pictures just to fill spaces)

- in general do not mix sans serif fonts in the same document

- in general do not mix serif fonts in the same document

Drawing and painting packages

Drawing and painting packages allow you to design, draw and manipulate pictures. They display symbols (icons) on the screen for the facilities (known as tools) available to create pictures. These tools include drawing and painting effects such as line drawing, paintbrushes, rollers, and spraycans. There are also colour palettes and a variety of controls for editing the whole picture or specified parts of it. Pictures can be scanned into a computer using a scanner which, when moved across a picture, produces a digitised image. These pictures can then be edited on the paint screen. Finished pictures can be printed in black and white, or, with an appropriate colour printer, in colour.

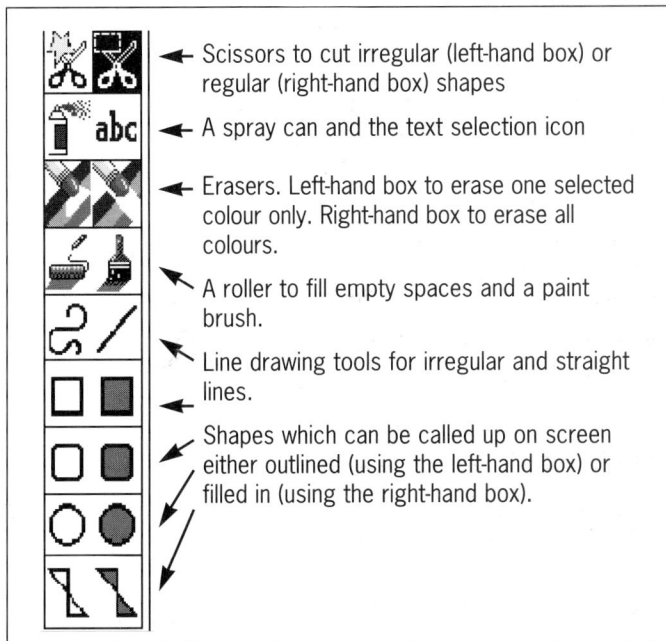

Scissors to cut irregular (left-hand box) or regular (right-hand box) shapes

A spray can and the text selection icon

Erasers. Left-hand box to erase one selected colour only. Right-hand box to erase all colours.

A roller to fill empty spaces and a paint brush.

Line drawing tools for irregular and straight lines.

Shapes which can be called up on screen either outlined (using the left-hand box) or filled in (using the right-hand box).

Figure 4

Figure 4 identifies the drawing, cutting and erasing tools found in most painting packages.

These icons are usually displayed down the left-hand side of the screen. Some painting packages may offer a greater range of tools such as graded colour merges, stretching effects for text, and curving effects for text.

Along the bottom of the screen is the colour palette (see Figure 5) which can be changed to grey shades when creating black and white images. In the bottom left-hand corner is a box in which you can select different line thicknesses.

Along the top of the page runs the menu bar with the names of the pull-down menus (FILE, EDIT, VIEW etc.). These are accessed by clicking on the words, using the mouse, and they offer you further facilities for manipulating your picture on the screen.

Below is an example of using the scissors tool to cut out part of a picture, and then, using the PICK pull-down menu, altering the cut portion by shrinking, flipping or tilting. The image begins with two masks (Figure 5).

The scissors are selected by moving the mouse to the icon and clicking. Then part of the image is selected by dragging the mouse across it. The PICK menu is

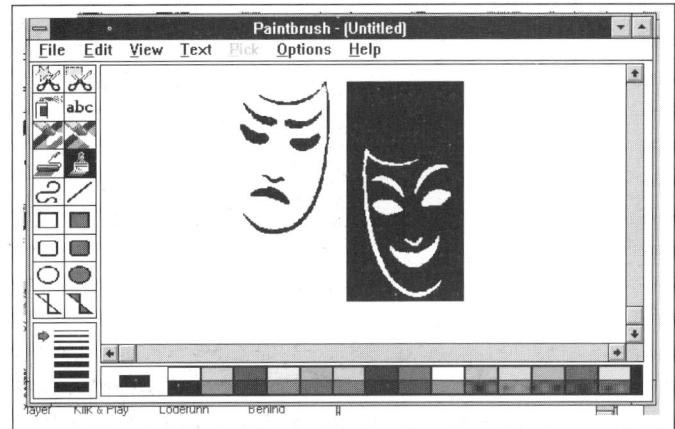

Figure 5

Figure 6

pulled down and the SHRINK & GROW option is selected (Figure 6).

A new area is now defined on the screen by dragging the mouse until the desired area is outlined with a dotted line. A copy of the mask's image appears there when the mouse button is released.

There are commands which allow the user to manipulate selected images. The entire image can be rotated, inverted, or switched horizontally to make a mirror image.

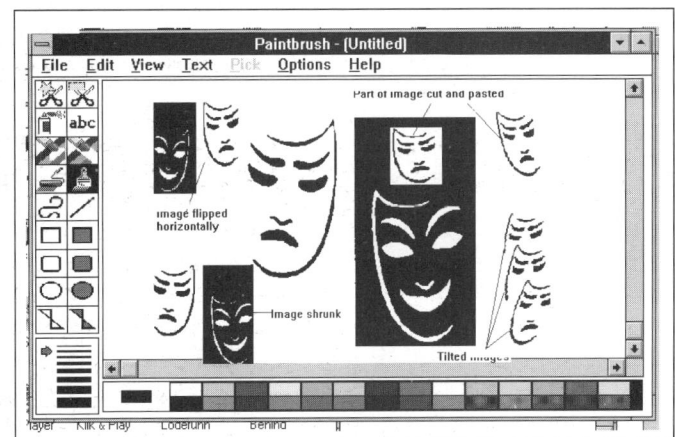

Figure 7

Clicking on the text icon enables text to be added to your image, and the TEXT pull-down menu (Figure 8) allows choices of fonts and point sizes to be made.

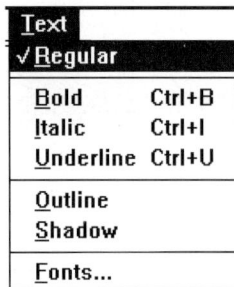

Figure 8

The FILE pull-down menu contains options to store, retrieve, preview and print your image.

Painting packages usually use 'bit-mapping' to store images. Everything on a screen is made up of pixels. A pixel is the smallest spot on a screen. With bit-mapping the computer stores an image by remembering where each pixel that makes up that image is located on the screen. If an image stored in this way is enlarged the computer simply increases the amount of pixels used to make up the image. This results in a fairly inaccurate image where the edges are jagged.

To overcome this problem there are more powerful drawing packages, such as *Corel Draw* and *Autocad,* which store images using vectors. This means every part of the image is stored as a mathematical equation describing its shape and position. The computer sees the equations that make up the image in relation to one another. If the size of an image created using vectors is changed the equations and relationships between them remain the same and therefore the image retains its accuracy and quality. CAD (Computer Aided Design) packages store images using vectors and are used in industries such as engineering, manufacturing and building to create three-dimensional diagrams which can be rescaled and viewed from different angles.

Designers who are creating detailed scaled drawings often use 'wire frame' drawing (see Figure 9). This means that they produce an outline of the image (see the left-hand drawing in Figure 9), which can be done fairly quickly and easily. The attributes of the various parts of the image can then be defined and the computer can use this information to fill in the wire frame using different levels of shading (see the right-hand drawing in Figure 9).

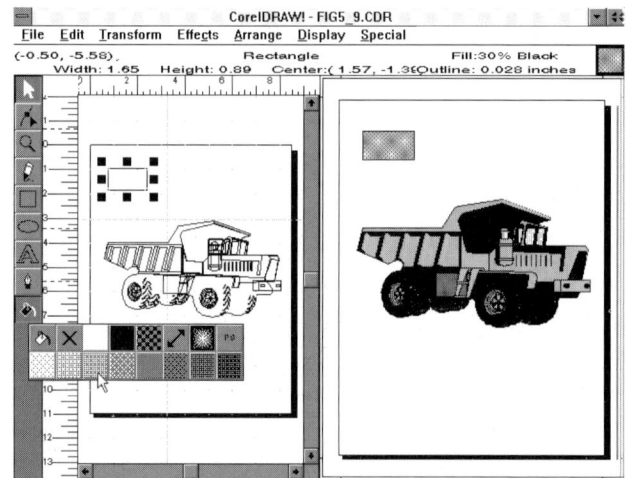

Figure 9

File management

Files

Files are collections of data that are stored in memory and can be recalled. There are many types of file such as:

- files that you create when you save your work

- files that control the start-up of the computer

- files which check that all is operating correctly when the computer starts-up.

- disk-operating-system files which, among other things, manage the storage, copying, moving, and deletion of other files

- application files which contain the information and data needed to run a particular package (or application)

> **Note** The term files is also used with databases; refer to page 98

It is not necessary to be aware of all the various types of file. Many of these files are to do with the computer's operating system and the applications that are running.

In general, you will only be concerned with the files that you create yourself and where and how those files are stored.

Naming files

Whenever you save a file you have to provide a unique name for that file. This name is then used by the disk operating system (DOS – which controls the setting up and basic running of a computer) to identify the file. There are a number of DOS systems, and they all require you to follow certain rules when naming files. All DOS systems are very similar and these rules vary very little between them. The most commonly found DOS system is MS-DOS (Microsoft Disk Operating System) which is the main DOS system used on IBM compatible personal computers. File names in MS-DOS are limited to eight characters, which can include numbers, letters and most keyboard characters (although some are reserved for special functions). Spaces cannot be used in filenames.

It is important to name your files clearly and in some sort of consistent style so that you can retrieve them easily. A poor name would be MYFILE because it gives you no indication of the content of the file. Whereas, the file name QUOTES3 is better because it gives you some clue about the contents (for example, this would be a third document containing quotes). Sometimes, more than one user accesses the same storage area and in these cases it is often useful to preface each file name with your initials. A common convention in this situation is to use a system which shows the initials of the person who created the file followed by a sequential reference number. For example someone called Isobel Bates might use IB71 to refer to the seventy-first document she has created.

Using file extensions

In addition to the eight characters allowed for in a file name there is an optional three-character extension which is separated from the rest by a full-stop.

The three-letter extension assists DOS in identifying different types of file. For example, .EXE or .BAT files can execute (run) themselves (they are used to start up the system), and .PCX, .TIF and .BMP are all graphics files of different formats.

Often extensions are inserted automatically by the package you are working in. A computer package which consists of many different components(such as a word processor, spreadsheet etc.) may use the extension to identify which component the file was created in. For example, .WKS for spreadsheets, .WDB for databases, and .BAK for backup copies of files. Sometimes such packages allow you to choose the extension. In these cases, you should use the appropriate extension for the area you created it in so that the computer knows what format it was created in and can read the data. For example, TASK1.TXT for a word processed document, TASK1.PCX for an image, TASK1.WKS for a spreadsheet, and TASK1.CHT for a chart.

Using wild cards in names

Although every file must have a unique name, it is not always necessary to specify the entire name when retrieving a file. DOS permits the use of the * character as a substitute for any other character or group of characters. Therefore, it is possible to specify part of a file name and substitute the rest with the * character, which will result in all file names with the characters you have specified and any further characters being retrieved. You can then carry out any command on these files. For example, retrieving *.DOC and deleting would result in all the files with the extension .DOC being deleted; retrieving MEMO*.* and printing would result in all the files beginning with MEMO and including other characters before or after the full stop (like MEMO1.DOC and MEMO2.TXT) being printed.

Directories

The hard disk of a machine may easily hold thousands of files, and a floppy disk can hold several hundred (depending on the size of the files). All the files on the hard disk are listed in the directory C:\ which may be likened to a filing cabinet. The

```
Root Directory (C:\)
          ├ Images
          ├ Database
          ├ Word Processor ┐ letters
                           ├ other documents
          ├ Spreadsheet
```

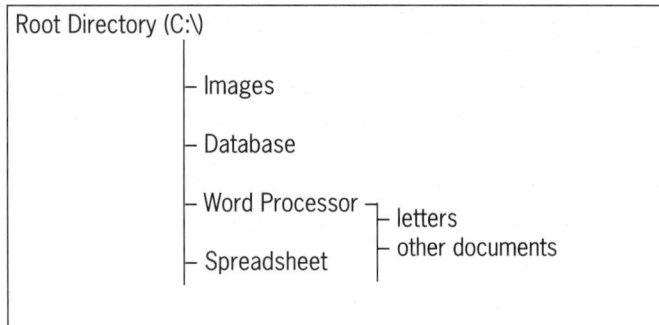

Figure 10   The 'tree' structure, with directories branching from the 'root' directory

directory may be so large that it would be easier to locate files if they were collected in smaller groups. Therefore, the disk operating system allows you to subdivide the directory into smaller directories that can be likened to different drawers in the filing cabinet. The large directory (the 'root directory') therefore has other directories branching off it, creating a 'tree' structure.

The same structure can be created on a floppy disk, where the root directory is A:\ . (If you have two disk drives one will be A:\ and the other B:\ .) The directories branching off the root directory can be subdivided to create further directories. This subdividing and branching off can be done as many times as you wish. However, if on trying to retrieve a file you have trouble remembering what directory you saved it in, you have probably created too many. Conversely, if you are having to search through dozens of files to find the right one, you probably have too few directories.

The root directory will usually contain some essential system files such as CONFIG.SYS and AUTOEXEC.BAT and also some hidden files such as IO.SYS. Branching from the root directory you may wish to create your directories to reflect different aspects of your work or your different assignments. Directories created in any package such as *Windows* or *Works* are branches off the root directory.

Housekeeping

It is often necessary to have a general 'tidy-up' of files. This is known as 'housekeeping'. Such operations are usually carried out in DOS. Table 2 below shows a few of the common DOS commands and their purpose.

It is often necessary to have a general 'tidy-up'......

Table 2

KEYSTROKES	RESULT
format A:	*formats disk in A drive*
dir/p	*displays the directory of files one page at a time*
dir	*lists files and sub-directories of the directory you are in*
diskcopy A: A:	*copies disk to disk using the A drive*
md WP	*makes a disk directory called WP*
move SOURCE WP\DOCS	*moves a file called SOURCE to the area of the disk called WP\DOCS*
copy SOURCE WP\DOCS	*copies a file called SOURCE to the area of the disk called WP\DOCS*
rename FILENAME.OLD FILENAME.NEW	*renames the file FILENAME.OLD to FILENAME.NEW*
del RUBBISH	*deletes a file called RUBBISH*
cls	*clears the screen*

A computer virus?......

The filenames in Table 2 have been shown in upper case. However, DOS is not case sensitive (it is irrelevant whether upper or lower case letters are used).

This is only a sample of the sorts of commands that one can utilise in DOS. It can become quite complicated, especially when incorporating detailed references to source and destination routes and paths.

File managers

All computers have disk operating systems which have facilities for file handling. The standard system for IBM-compatible computers is MS-DOS. While creating directories, and copying, moving and deleting files can be carried out using DOS commands, you need to be experienced in DOS to use those commands effectively. It is usually more convenient to use a specialised file management program to carry out typical housekeeping jobs.

File management programs allow those not familiar with DOS commands to sort out their files using simple instructions. For example, a file manager enables you to mark the files required from a list and then copy or move them to a new destination, often by just dragging and dropping them in their new location. A file manager also provides powerful options for removing whole branches of the tree structure, including directories which still contain files.

Protecting files

If you do not wish other people to add data to your files, they can be made 'read only', or, if you do not want anyone else to even see them, they can be 'hidden'. These options can be applied to any identified files, and may be done through DOS or a file manager program.

You may wish to make a whole disk read-only, and this is done by covering the notch on the right hand side of a 5.25″ disk or by moving the plastic write protect slide upwards on a 3.5″ disk so that a small hole is revealed.

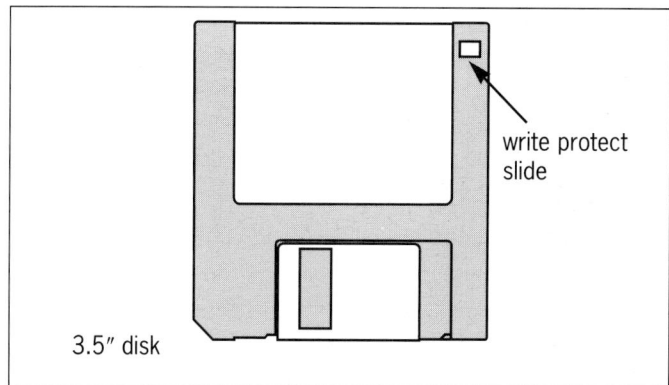

write protect slide

3.5″ disk

Figure 11

If you wish to save data to files you have protected, you must first cancel the protection.

Viruses

A computer virus is a piece of software that, if it gets into your computer, can damage work that you have done. It is like an infectious disease and is usually spread from one computer to another through contaminated disks. The damage they cause ranges from flashing messages on the screen to the destruction of entire contents of hard disks. It is important to check that your disks are not contaminated. Some file manager programs have virus checking facilities, otherwise these are available as additional programs.

Graphs and charts

Graphs are used to present numerical data in a way which is easy for the reader to interpret and understand at a glance. Graphs are commonly used in business. There are different sorts of graphs and, depending on your data, one sort may be more suitable than another. Pie charts show the proportions of a set of figures. Bar charts and line graphs show trends of increasing or decreasing activity. Graphs are often used to compare one set of figures with another. Below is a pie chart showing the percentage of each component in a budget.

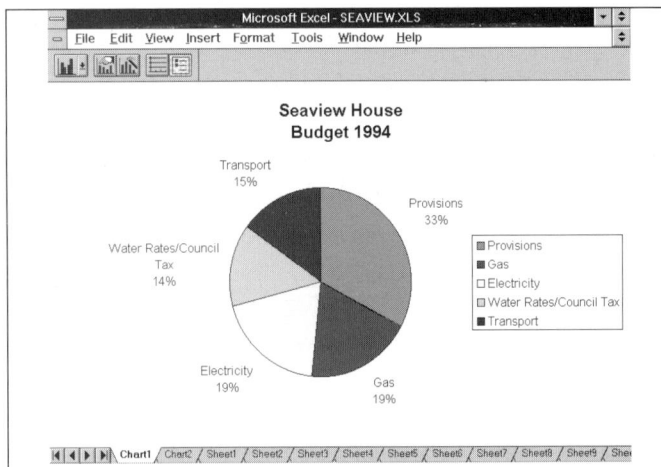

Figure 12

Graphs can be produced from data in a spreadsheet. Some spreadsheet packages have charting facilities through which you can specify which type of graph you require and which elements of the spreadsheet you want to represent in the graph. The package will produce the graph for you and may even be able to interpret the data. If your spreadsheet package does not have these facilities you will have to use a separate graphing package and all the data will have to be inputted into this.

Below are some of the terms commonly used to describe different parts of a bar chart or line graph.

X-AXIS: This is the horizontal axis of the chart.

X-SERIES: This refers to the labels along the X-axis. In a bar chart these explain what each bar represents.

Y-AXIS: This is the vertical axis of the chart.

Y-SERIES: This refers to the numerical range extending up the Y-axis. A chart may have several Y-series. In this situation they are named the FIRST Y-SERIES, SECOND Y-SERIES, etc.

LEGENDS: These are the labels which refer to each type of bar or each line in the graph. They are needed when a different pattern, colour or style is used for bars or lines, and there is no room within the graph itself to describe them. They are shown using a key.

TITLES: A main title, subtitle, and titles to label the X- and Y-axes of the chart can be supplied. These can come from certain cell references on a spreadsheet or be inputted separately.

Below is an example of a spreadsheet with the information required to create a graph identified by highlighted cells.

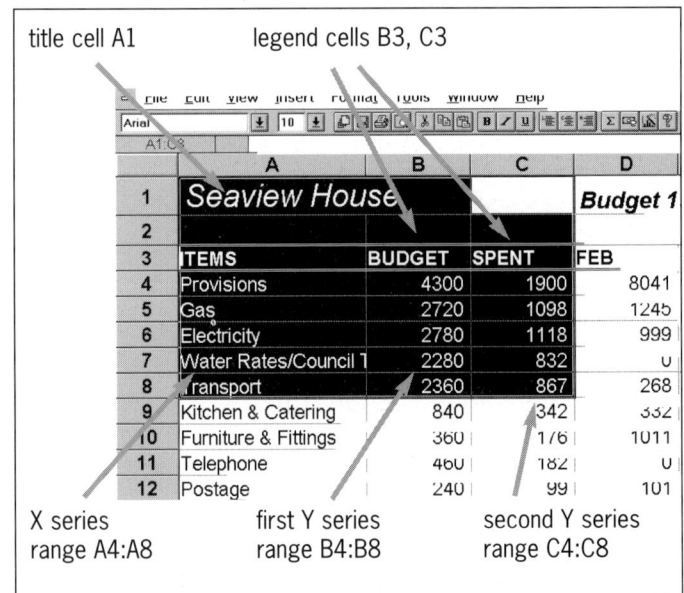

Figure 13

Figure 14 shows this selection of information in a bar chart.

If your package produces a graph which is not exactly what you require you can change it. The X- and Y-series can be redefined, the legends and titles changed (including the font used) and the type of graph and its layout reselected. This can be achieved in some packages by using the pull-down menus where

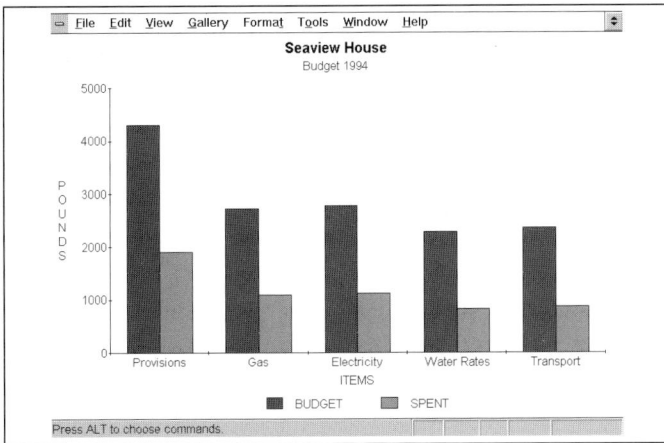

Figure 14

A line graph is useful to indicate trends which have occurred over a certain period, or to compare trends from different periods. An example of a line graph comparing the number of guests at Seaview House during July 1993 with the number during July 1994 is shown in Figure 18. The information to create it was taken from the spreadsheet data in Figure 17.

	A	B	C	D	E
1	Seaview House		Guests		
2	July	Week 1	Week 2	Week 3	Week 4
3	1993	222	230	282	320
4	1994	235	270	250	334
5					
6					
7					

Figure 17

options for different graph types and layouts can be found. In other packages there is a bar across the top of the screen, such as the one in Figure 15, offering you choices for different types of graph.

From this selection of data the spreadsheet package interpreted (correctly) that the row containing the weeks (row 2) was to be the X-SERIES labels, that the cells A3 and A4 from the first column were to be the legend text, and that the rows ranging from B3 to E3 and B4 to E4 were to be interpreted as the two Y-SERIES.

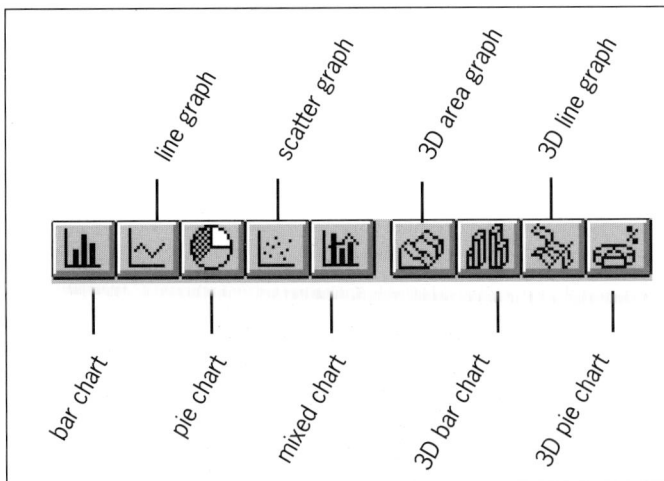

Figure 15

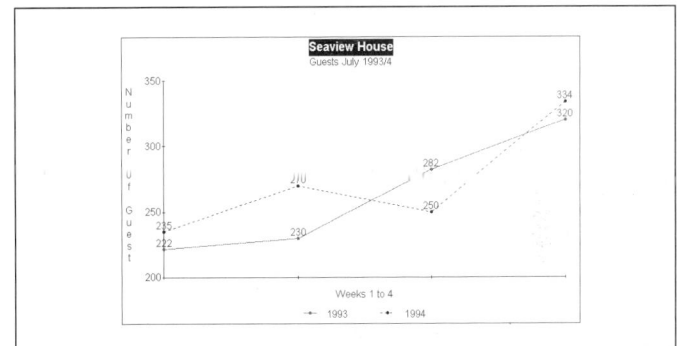

Figure 18

3D graphs can help to make your presentation of information more dynamic. Figure 16 is an example of a 3D bar chart.

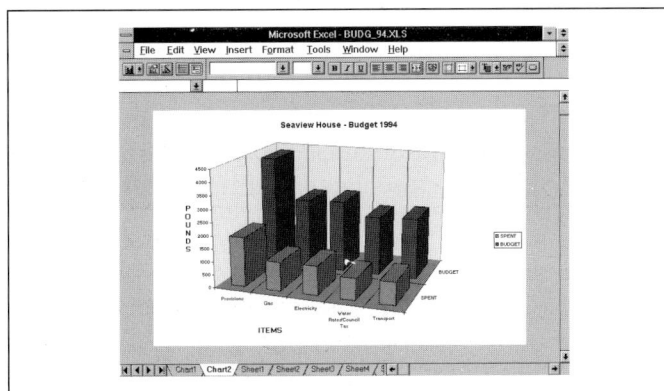

Figure 16

The graph was then edited using the pull-down menus. The Y-axis has been altered so the lowest number (where the Y-axis meets the X-axis) is 200 rather than 0, as the lowest number to be mapped on the graph is 222. This has brought the X-axis closer to the lines on the graph and makes the graph clearer and easier to interpret. The highest number has been altered to 350, so it is just above the largest number to be mapped on the graph. A border has also been drawn around the graph which gives it a more finished effect.

Spreadsheets

A spreadsheet is a type of program which uses tables to store and manipulate data. The main use of a spreadsheet is the calculation and recalculation of numbers. Spreadsheets are typically used for financial projections (e.g. testing new business ventures, projecting the sales for a new product), budget control (e.g. calculating the cost of a holiday), keeping track of the cost of a project, cost analysis (e.g. analysis of a past project); but there are many other uses. Many organisations use spreadsheets, instead of databases, to store and sort data.

The simple spreadsheet below shows a record of daily expenditure:

Figure 19

Looking at Figure 19, you will see that the row across the top of the grid shows the references to the columns underneath (A, B, C, etc) and that the column at the left shows the references to the rows across (1, 2, 3, etc). The smallest single unit on a spreadsheet is known as a cell. Each cell has a unique reference (e.g. B2, F8).

A table such as that above shows:

- the amount spent on a particular item on a particular day (for example pub expenditure for Saturday is located in cell E7)

- the total daily expenditure for each item (the spending for each day is in the rows across)

- the total expenditure on each item for the week (the spending for each item is in the columns down)

- the total weekly expenditure (G9)

One of the most powerful aspects of a spreadsheet is its ability to instantly calculate and recalculate rows and columns of figures. The totals are derived by using formulas. Once the formulas are in the spreadsheet, the calculations are done automatically. For instance, if you enter a formula into a cell that adds up all the cells above it, you will be able to change a value in any of those cells and the total will change automatically.

The example in Figure 19 displays totals along the bottom and along the right-hand side. This is fairly common in spreadsheets. Note that the total of the numbers in the bottom row equals the total of the numbers in the column on the far right.

Spreadsheets can store a huge amount of data, although you can only see a screen at a time. The screen can be thought of as a window, through which you are able to have a partial view. Large spreadsheets cannot be viewed in their totality. Indeed, their size is such that, if the calculations were to be done on paper, it would be necessary to spread the sheets of paper out over a large surface. Hence the term 'spreadsheet'. On paper, the alteration of one number could result in a great deal of recalculation involving many different numbers and totals. The beauty of a spreadsheet program is that if any changes are made, all the calculations, throughout the spreadsheet, are automatically adjusted.

Creating a spreadsheet

If you are designing a spreadsheet from scratch you will need to know more than just how to enter data and formulas. You need to be familiar with the profession which is seeking to use the spreadsheet and the context in which it is to be used. For example, if you are going to create a spreadsheet which generates mathematical tables it will help if you understand the associated mathematical principles.

Many people waste a huge amount of time on spreadsheets because they have not planned the design properly. Do not enter any data until the design and purpose for your spreadsheet is clear.

If spreadsheet calculations were done on paper it would be necessary to spread the sheets over a large surface.

Entering data

First of all, you need to select on screen the cell in which you are going to enter your data. Use the cursor keys on your keyboard, or your mouse, to move around the spreadsheet to the selected cell. Note, as you are moving around the spreadsheet, that the precise location of your cursor is displayed at the top left-hand corner of the screen. The selected cell will be highlighted. Each cell is referred to by its column and row.

Remember that there may be much of the spreadsheet which does not appear in your 'window'. Therefore, you may have to move your window around until the particular area of the spreadsheet you require is shown.

When you are entering the data into the cell, it will be displayed on what is known as the command line (see Figure 20). The data may also appear in the cell itself. When the data in the command line is as you require press the enter key. The data should now appear in the highlighted cell.

There are three main types of data you can enter:

Numeric data

All you have to do is enter the numbers, and associated features, such as decimal points.

Labels

You will have to enter some type of description for each column and row. These are called labels. They are essential as it is very difficult to make sense of a spreadsheet without them. Text is generally used for labels, but numbers or dates can be included. It is common practice to place the labels for the rows down the left-hand side of the spreadsheet. If the text is too long for a cell it will overflow into the next one.

Formulas

A formula is a mathematical equation. It is entered into the cell in which the answer is required. The formula carries out one or more calculations. The most common calculations are:

Addition

Subtraction

Multiplication

Division

The formula will normally include references to other cells which hold the numerical data. It is necessary to indicate that the data about to be entered is a formula. Therefore, the entry must start with a symbol, which is usually an equals sign, e.g. = B5+B6 (meaning 'this cell equals the value in B5 plus the value in B6').

Symbol	Purpose	Example	Explanation
+	add	D4+D5	adds the number in cell D4 to the number in cell D5
−	subtract	7–D5	takes the contents of cell D5 away from the number 7
*	multiply	D4*D5	multiplies the number in cell D4 by the number in D5
/	divide	D5/D4	divides D5 by D4

Table 3

The menu

All spreadsheets have menus from which options can be selected. If there is no menu bar – a line across the top of the spreadsheet displaying the menu names – the menus can usually be accessed by using the / key.

Changing appearances

There will probably be occasions when you will want to change the layout of a spreadsheet. Most changes involve a standard process:

- highlighting the cell, column or row to be altered
- selecting the FORMAT command from the menu
- selecting the display required

There are many different ways of showing numbers. They can be aligned to the left, aligned to the right or centred. They can show decimal points or be whole numbers (integers). Other numeric formats include date, percentages and scientific display. (As on a calculator, scientific display allows you to display very large numbers exactly.)

It is also useful to be able to manipulate the alignment of labels (i.e. aligned to the left, aligned to the right or centred). On most spreadsheets, text and numbers can also be highlighted, emboldened and displayed in italic format.

Columns and rows can be narrowed, widened or moved using the mouse or commands from the FORMAT menu.

Internal precision

What appears on the screen may not be presented exactly as you entered it. The way the information is displayed in the spreadsheet depends upon the formatting of the cell. For instance, if you enter the number 6.3, it may appear as 6.3. However, in the integer format it would appear as 6 (the number is rounded to the nearest whole number) and in the decimal format it would appear as 6.30. In practice, the number that you entered, in this case 6.3, is still there. The change in appearance does not affect the spreadsheets internal precision. Any calculation would be based upon the entered number and not on what appears on the screen.

Common functions

There are various types of pre-defined instructions within a spreadsheet program which can be used to execute a process. These are called functions. Most spreadsheet functions are concerned with mathematical, statistical and financial calculations.

Take, for example, a row of items. This could be totalled by the following entry into a cell:
=D3+D4+D5+D6+D7+D8+D9+D10+D11

But there is also a function called the SUM function, which serves this purpose more quickly.

The same result could be achieved by entering =SUM(D3.D11) which tells the program to add all the figures in row D between, and inclusive of, D3 and D11. Although the format of the function may vary slightly between spreadsheets – some separate the two cell references with a colon, e.g. =SUM(D3:D11) and others use two dots, e.g. =SUM(D3..D11) – the principle is the same.

There are many such functions, and they can be extremely sophisticated. The more common examples include SUM (which adds up all the numbers in the specified cells), COUNT (which counts the number of cells), MIN (which finds the smallest number in the specified cells), and AVERAGE (which finds the average of the specified cells).

For additional help you will need to refer to the appropriate manuals or other documentation.

Copying and replication

Copying and moving data from one part of a spreadsheet to another can be done by highlighting and copying the data, and then pasting it into another area. You can also use the fill facility to highlight the cell you wish to copy and then to mark any adjacent cells, which will be filled with the data from the highlighted cell.

'Replication' is a specific form of copying, commonly associated with spreadsheets. It is the name given to copying formulas. Look at the extract in Figure 20 of the spreadsheet shown previously.

B9	↓	=SUM(B2:B8)	command line	
	A	**B**	**C**	**D**	**E**
		Food	Travel	Lodgings	Pub
1					
2	Monday	0	0.72	0	0
3	Tuesday	2.09	0.72	0	0
4	Wednesday	1.98	0.72	0	0
5	Thursday	2.15	0.72	0	0
6	Friday	2	0.72	0	7.12
7	Saturday	0	0	35	14.5
8	Sunday	0	0	0	1.72
9	Totals	=SUM(B2:B8)			
10					

Figure 20

We can see that in cell B9 the formula for the food total is =SUM(B2:B8). When the formula is copied to C9, the references to the cells will automatically change to C, i.e. =SUM(C2.C8). This is an example of relational replication; in other words the relationship between the row and column in the formula is replicated and the cell references are automatically adjusted to fit in with the new position of the formula.

In some cases it is necessary to ensure that an item in a formula will remain the same regardless of the formula's position in the spreadsheet, as it is a figure that is constant (e.g. the VAT rate). Therefore, the cell reference for that item must not change when the formula is moved around. To achieve this, it is necessary to use 'absolute referencing', which ensures that both the relationship *and* the actual cell references are copied. An absolute reference to a cell is marked by using a dollar sign before the letter and the number in the cell reference (e.g. =A1 is an absolute reference to cell A1). Some formulas may contain a constant figure alongside figures that should change in relation to the position of the formula in the spreadsheet. It is possible to use both relational and absolute referencing for these formulas (see page 72).

Printing

Spreadsheets can be printed out by means of the PRINT facility which is available from the menu line. Normally, the PRINT option will assume you want the whole spreadsheet printed out.

Often spreadsheets do not fit easily on to one sheet of paper. Here are some possible solutions:

- print the spreadsheet sideways (landscape), which might enable a wide table to fit on a sheet of paper

- condense the print/type size

- select and print a part only

The PRINT option usually offers the facility to produce graphical information – for example, converting data into pie charts, bar charts, stacked bar charts or line graphs (see *Graphs and charts* p. 110 for examples).

Another important facility is to be able to print out the spreadsheet formulas. This helps in analysing the spreadsheet, seeing the relationships between cells and functions, and detecting potential flaws.

Other facilities

Protecting cells

It is possible to protect a spreadsheet, which stops anyone being able to alter the data. Usually, it will only be necessary to protect part of your spreadsheet. Protection is a particularly useful facility if the spreadsheet is to be used by other people. For example, a manager may use a spreadsheet to forecast profits and losses. The cells which contain known costs could be protected so that only the estimated and forecasted figures could be altered.

Finding cells

There are different ways of moving around and finding data on spreadsheets. As always, the facilities of different spreadsheet packages vary slightly, but there are two common ways of finding data. One is to use a 'goto' facility, where you specify the reference of the cell you wish to find. The other is to use a search facility (which works in the same way as the search on a word processor or a database) for which you specify the characteristics of the data you want to find, and the program highlights the cell or cells which contain that data.

Hiding cells

It is sometimes the case that confidential information needs to be used in a spreadsheet but must not be seen by many of the users (for example, the salaries of a company's employees). Therefore, it is possible to hide the contents of specified cells. This is one way of protecting data from unauthorised or accidental change.

Macros

If you find you are regularly repeating the same sequence of commands, then you may find it helpful to create a macro. This is a way of recording a sequence of commands and programming it to be initiated by only one command. For example, you could create a macro to always generate the company name in a particular typeface and point size and call up the date in a particular cell. Macros can also be used in other programs, such as databases, DTP programs and word processing programs.

In the checklist below, fill in the keystrokes you need to do in order to use the facilities listed down the left-hand side.

Personal SPREADSHEET checklist

Facility	Keystrokes
Align left	
Align right	
Change column width	
Enter formula	
Enter numeric labels	
Exit program	
Extend the spreadsheet	
Generate date	
Goto specified cell	
Graphs	
Insert row/column	

Facility	Keystrokes
Integer format (whole numbers)	
Mark (highlight) data	
Print	
Print formulas	
Print graphs	
Protect data	
Recalculate (generate new values)	
Replicate (copy)	
Save	
Show formulas	

Windows

Windows is a GUI (Graphical User Interface). The most common windows package is Microsoft Windows. Any programs that are run within Windows look similar, and are used in similar ways. When you use a program in Windows it runs in a rectangular box called a window and is set on a background called a desktop.

Program manager

Windows is most commonly opened through DOS by typing WIN at the command line. When you start Windows the Program Manager appears. It always runs when you are in Windows, and through it you can see what applications are available, and access them. In Windows, the applications you have on your computer are represented by icons. To access an application you need to double-click with the left-hand mouse button on the icon. Usually, within Program Manager, applications are placed together in groups, and the group icon is displayed. You need to open the correct group to access an application. Figure 21 shows some programs commonly available within Windows and their associated icons.

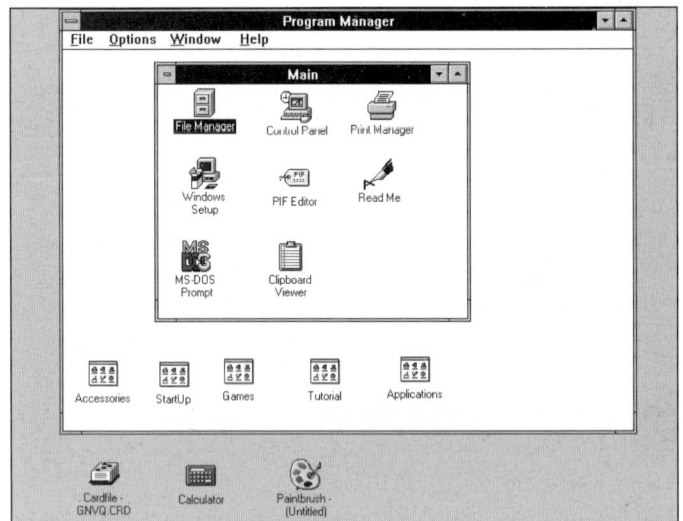

Figure 21

The control line

In the top left-hand corner of a window is the control box (see Figure 22). Clicking once on this produces a pull-down menu of options to change the size of the window. As with all pull-down menus in Windows, the options in bold can be choosen by dragging the mouse down to that option and releasing the button. Any options shown in grey cannot be chosen. Double clicking in the control box shuts down the window and the application running in it.

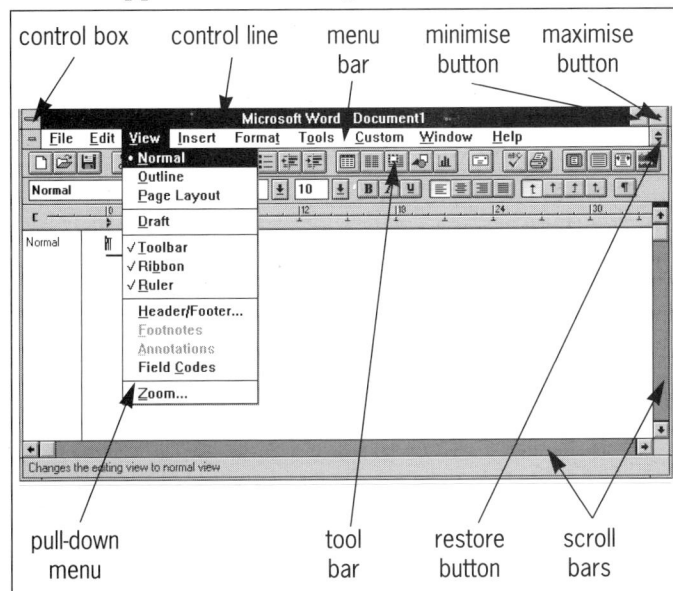

Figure 22

Along the top of the window the name of the application that is running within it is displayed. In the top right-hand corner there are two boxes. If you click on the one with a down-turned arrow the window will be minimised into an icon (this is the minimise button), but the application will still be running. If you click in the box with the up-turned arrow the window will maximise and fill the whole screen (this is the maximise button) - other windows can still be open behind it. Sometimes there is a box which contains both a down-turned arrow and an up-turned arrow, which will restore the window to its previous size. The size of your window can also be changed by taking the mouse to the bottom corner of the window, clicking the left-hand button, and dragging the corner out to create a larger window or in to create a smaller one, then releasing the button.

Pull-down menus

The next line down in a window (often known as the menu bar) contains a series of pull-down menus. Clicking on a word here with the left-hand mouse button will display a menu (see Figure 22). Dragging the mouse down the menu until the required option is highlighted, and then releasing the mouse button, will select that option.

Option icons

Sometimes there is a line below this in a window (often known as a toolbar) which contains several icons which represent some of the options within the pull-down menus. By clicking on one of these icons the option is selected without the need to pull down a menu.

Scroll bars

Along the bottom and right-hand edge of a window are the scroll bars. These can be used to move your document up, down, or to the left or right, if the whole document cannot be viewed in the window. On the bars are small boxes. The one in the right-hand bar can be dragged up to see further up in the document, or down to see further on in the document. The one in the scroll bar across the bottom of the window can be moved across to the right or left to enable the whole width of the document to be viewed. This is achieved by clicking on the box with the left-hand mouse button, dragging the box along the scroll bar, and releasing the button.

Alternatively, you can click on the arrows at the end of the scroll bars which will scroll you through the document. You could also move through your document by using the page up and page down keys on your keyboard.

The help facilities

Windows programs generally have a help facility. There is often a HELP pull-down menu. The help

you will need to select the appropriate option from the menu.....

offered through this menu usually relates to the application that you are working in at the time. From Program Manager you can choose options from the HELP menu which teach you about Windows and how to use a mouse.

Opening several windows

In Windows you can have more than one application running at a time, rather than having to quit one to open another. Therefore, you could be working in one and printing from another. This ability to use several programs at the same time is called 'multi-tasking'.

Because you have more than one window open at a time, you can view more than one application at a time. These windows can be arranged so that they all have an equal proportion of the screen (tiling them), or so that they sit one on top of another with just a small piece of each showing (cascading them). You can only work in one window at a time, but you can swap between them simply by clicking anywhere within the window you want to use. Information can easily be exchanged between applications by opening the relevant applications and copying and pasting between the windows. There are other ways of exchanging information such as DDE (Dynamic Data Exchange) and OLE (Object Linking and Embedding), which create live data links between the applications.

Word processors

A word-processing program allows you to enter and manipulate text on screen and subsequently to print out the text. Word-processing programs are designed to make it easier to produce clear documents. As people and organisations often have to produce written material – for example, essays, reports, memorandums, articles, publicity materials – it is not surprising that word-processing is the most commonly used application on business and personal computers.

Word-processing facilities allow you to enter text, to insert, delete and make corrections to text, and to change the appearance and size of the document. Word-processing allows you to create:

Different HEADINGS

It enables you to make the text **bold**, *italic* or underlined. Text and headings can be

aligned to the left

aligned to the right

or centred.

Text can also be 'justified' which means that each line is aligned to the left and the right. The program achieves this by adjusting the spacing between words.

The type face can be altered **and the size changed to create different appearances.**

More than one column can be created on the page allowing you to make the text look like a newspaper or to list various items alongside one another.

A page number can be shown at the top or bottom of the page and aligned to the left or right or centred. The one on this page is situated at the top and is aligned to the left. (Aligned to the left or right is often referred to as justified to the left or right.)

One of the shortcomings of the first word-processing packages was that the way the text was displayed on the screen was not how it appeared when printed. Then desktop publishing packages (DTP) were produced that displayed the text on screen exactly as it would print out; this facility is known as 'WYSIWYG' – which stands for 'What You See Is What You Get'. It is now common to find this facility in the more powerful word-processing packages, but these require powerful computers on which to operate. Many of the other facilities of DTP are now included in word-processing packages, such as the ability to put text in columns, to draw diagrams and graphs, and to use different print types and sizes. Conversely, many people use a desktop publishing package mainly for word-processing. (Hence DTP programs are increasingly incorporating word-processing facilities.)

Entering and manipulating text

The best way to begin to learn about word-processing is to play around with a dummy document. You need to get into a word-processing program and open up a blank document. Then try:

- entering some lines of text
- moving around with the cursor keys (and/or a mouse if there is one)
- deleting words
- inserting words

You will notice that if a word will not fit at the end of one line it will be forced on to the next. This is called 'wrap-around'. When the end of a line has been reached this facility automatically moves the text on to the next line. (Furthermore, the wordprocessor will determine when one page should end and will begin a new one. This is called 'pagination'.)

On a typewriter you have to press the carriage return at the end of every line to take you to the beginning of the next line. This is not necessary in a word-processing package, when typing in continuous text, because of the wrap-around facility. (The carriage return on a keyboard is commonly known as the ENTER key.) The ENTER key should only be used if you want to advance on to a new line before reaching the end of the one you are on, e.g. for a new paragraph.

If you wish to manipulate several words, or larger sections of text – for example, to move, underline or delete them – then you can mark or highlight ('block') the section and then carry out the appropriate commands. The command will be implemented in the whole of the highlighted section. If it is not apparent how to mark or highlight the text you can:

- use the program's help facilities (most programs have these)
- look at reference documentation (e.g. worksheets or the manual)
- ask somebody else

While you are learning, fill in the checklist at the end of this section and use it for reference.

Templates (style sheets)

If you use a particular style of document frequently, you can save time and effort by setting a template or style sheet. Any part of the document that is always the same is saved in a file and can be retrieved when you want to create one of these documents. You can store such things as headings, paragraphs styles, screen layouts and macros in your template. (see p. 104)

Formatting the layout

Indent
Indenting the text inserts a space between the margin and the text. This can be used for just one line (e.g. the first line of a paragraph that needs to be set in from the left-hand margin) or for a number of lines. Indenting text from the left and the right can be particularly useful for quotes, to make them stand out from the main body of the text. Text can also be indented from some kind of reference point,

such as a letter or number, and this is called a 'hanging indent'.

Indent:	Hanging Indent:
The employee handbook lists the terms and conditions of employment and can be obtained from the personnel department. In her speech the Managing Director said: "The success of the company over the last year has been entirely due to the hardworking and committed workforce."	1) Holiday forms must be authorised by your Manager. 2) A copy of the form must be sent to the personnel department.

Tabs

The term 'tabs' is an abbreviation for tabulations. These are a series of points that are marked across the page and are moved to by using the tab key. It is possible to indent and line up text using the tabs. A word-processing program will automatically set the tabs across the page (the default setting) but you can re-set the tabs to the distances you require.

Personal WORD PROCESSOR checklist

Facility	Keystrokes
Align left	_____
Align right	_____
Change format	_____
Change margins	_____
Delete text	_____
Exit program	_____
Go to beginning of document	_____
Go to end of document	_____
Help facility	_____
Insert	_____
Justify (align left and right)	_____
Mark (highlight) text	_____
New page	_____
Overwrite	_____
Print	_____
Save document	_____
Search and replace	_____
Spell check	_____
Tabs	_____
Undo	_____

Other features

The diagram below highlights the features found in a good word-processing program.

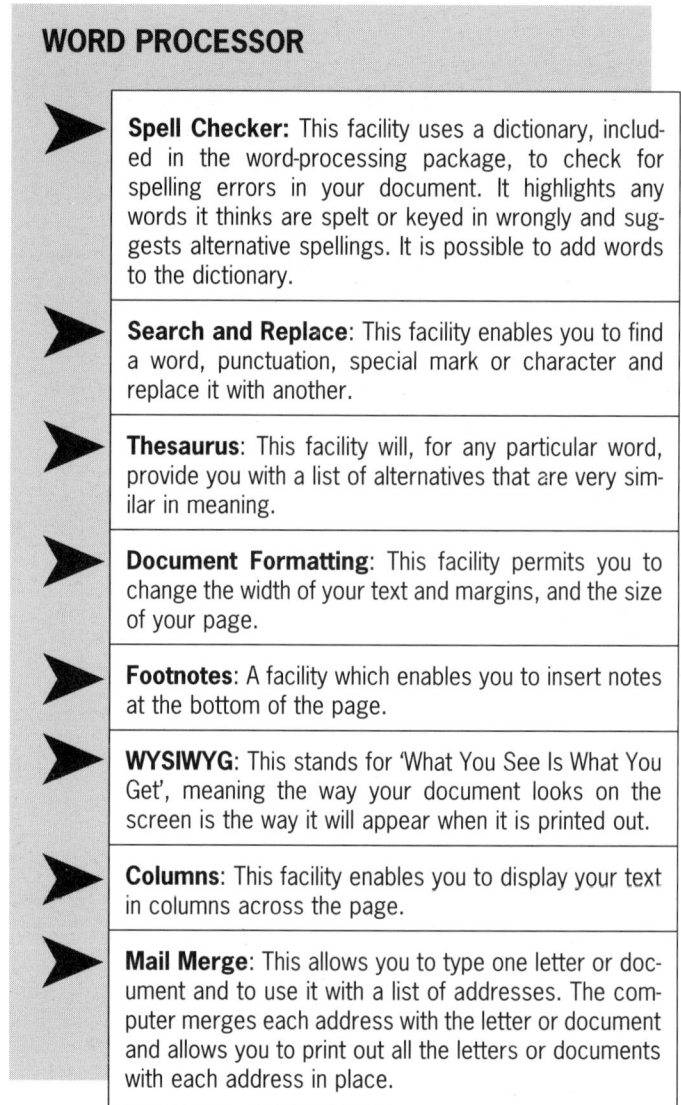

WORD PROCESSOR

➤ **Spell Checker:** This facility uses a dictionary, included in the word-processing package, to check for spelling errors in your document. It highlights any words it thinks are spelt or keyed in wrongly and suggests alternative spellings. It is possible to add words to the dictionary.

➤ **Search and Replace:** This facility enables you to find a word, punctuation, special mark or character and replace it with another.

➤ **Thesaurus:** This facility will, for any particular word, provide you with a list of alternatives that are very similar in meaning.

➤ **Document Formatting:** This facility permits you to change the width of your text and margins, and the size of your page.

➤ **Footnotes:** A facility which enables you to insert notes at the bottom of the page.

➤ **WYSIWYG:** This stands for 'What You See Is What You Get', meaning the way your document looks on the screen is the way it will appear when it is printed out.

➤ **Columns:** This facility enables you to display your text in columns across the page.

➤ **Mail Merge:** This allows you to type one letter or document and to use it with a list of addresses. The computer merges each address with the letter or document and allows you to print out all the letters or documents with each address in place.

Glossary

Absolute and Relative Referencing

In *spreadsheet* packages, a formula from one cell may need to be duplicated to other cells. Either just the formula is replicated in another cell, and the cell references are changed to fit in with the formula's new position (relative referencing), or the formula including the actual cell references is replicated (absolute referencing). (see page 115)

Accounting Packages

Business accounting packages are used to record and analyse financial transactions. At the heart of general accounting packages are three sets of accounts, known as ledgers. These are the 'sales ledger', the 'purchase ledger' and the 'nominal ledger'. Accounting packages can produce various specialised reports from the *data*, such as statements for overdue accounts. Sophisticated packages can contain more specific ledgers such as payroll and stock control.

Applications

These are *programs* that carry out specific tasks. *Word processors*, *spreadsheets* and *databases* are all applications.

ASCII

An acronym for American Standard Code for Information Interchange - pronounced 'ASKEY'. It is used for the transmission of *data* between different *programs* or between machines.

Automated Routines

These are a means of programming a series of steps and initiating them automatically. They are useful for functions that need to be repeated several times. Examples include *macros*, programmable keys and icons, mail-merge, database query and report routines. (see *Procedures*)

Back-Up

A spare copy of a *program* or *data* which can be retrieved if the original is destroyed or spoiled. (see page 65)

BASIC

This is an acronym for Beginners All Symbolic Instruction Code. This is a programming language which was created in order to make programming on a computer easier. One line is inputted at a time, and is checked by the computer before the next line can be accepted.

Batch Files

These are used to store series of instructions which perform commonly needed functions (e.g. starting up a *program*). With a batch file, you can execute the instructions by typing in the name of the batch file rather than having to enter each individual instruction.

Binary

Computers use the binary number system which only has two components, 0 and 1. In *computers*, all information is recorded as a series of electrical pulses, represented by combinations of 0 (electricity off) and 1 (electricity on).

Bit

One of the two digits 0 or 1, used in *binary* notation.

Byte

Universally taken to mean a string of 8 *bits*. Various combinations of 8 *bits* enable any integer (whole) number between 0 and 255 to be stored. Each *ASCII* character code requires one byte for storage.

Kilobytes (often abbreviated as 'K'), *megabytes* and

gigabytes are all units for expressing quantities of *data* in bytes.

1 kilobyte = 1,024 bytes, but increasingly being used to mean 1000 bytes.

1 Megabytes (MB) = 1,024 kilobytes

1 Gigabyte (GB) = 1,024 megabytes = 1,048,576 kilobytes

Cache Memory

An area of *RAM* that is much faster to read from, and write to, than normal *RAM*. It is used for storing the most frequently, and the most recently used portions of the currently running *program* in anticipation that they may be required in the near future. Cache memory can dramatically increase the speed at which a *program* runs. It is, however, very expensive to purchase which is why it is not used for the entire *RAM*.

CAD

An acronym for Computer-Aided Design (Drawing or Drafting). CAD is an application used for design that simulates a draftsman's drawing board and instruments. It can be used to produce three-dimensional diagrams which can then be rescaled and viewed from different angles.

CD-ROM

CD-ROM stands for Compact Disc Read Only Memory. CD-ROMs look just like music CDs. Although the uses of CD-ROMs vary enormously, the one common feature is the ability to store vast quantities of *data* (650MB) that can be accessed readily. However, the access time for *hard disks* is still much faster than for CD-ROMs.

Central Processing Unit (CPU)

The chip, or series of chips, which have ultimate control of a computer. There are three parts to a CPU: a store; an arithmetic logic unit; and a control unit. The CPU executes all *program* instructions.

Clipboard

A clipboard is a temporary storage area for *data*. It allows you to copy *data* from one application and place it in another.

Communications

See *Telecommunications*

Compatibility

The ability of different types of *software* and *hardware* to work together. This means *data* produced in one type can be read on a different type.

Computer

A machine that accepts, processes, and outputs *data* according to a set of instructions. It is not a thinking machine, but can be programmed to make decisions, or calculate numbers or results, by comparing and acting upon *data* received.

Computer System

A computer system consists of a *computer* and all its attachments, actions, inputs and outputs, when considered as a whole.

Configure

The process by which a computer and its parts are customised for a particular user, organisation or country. The final set up of the computer is termed its 'configuration'. Most of the common *software applications* can be configured.

Cursor

An indicator on the screen that shows you where the next character, number or image will be entered.

Data and Information

Data is anything that has been inputted into a computer. A computer can only process data. Information is data that is understood by a human being. For instance, the number 250646 stored in a computer is data, and only becomes information when someone understands what it signifies – in this case it is a telephone number.

Data Protection Act

This Act, which was passed in 1984, gives all individuals the right to know all the information held on a computer that relates to them (with some exceptions, such as police or medical records). If necessary, individuals may request corrections to be made. All companies and organisations which hold computerised *data* about individuals are obliged to register with the Data Protection Registrar as a 'data user'. The onus is on the individual to locate any computer holding information relevant to themselves if they wish to request it. Organisations that receive such requests must respond within 40 days, and give all the information held on the computer, for which they may charge a fee.

Database

An application that stores *data* and can be used to sort and retrieve that *data* in many different ways. (see page 98)

Datalogging

A method of electronically collecting *data* which can be subsequently processed and analysed by a computer. Datalogging is used widely - for example, for recording weather variations, counting traffic, and in many types of scientific experiments.

The Data Protection Act gives everyone the right to know all information held on computer that relates to them.

Desktop Publishing (DTP)

This is a type of program which can be used to produce high-quality documents with close attention to detail. (see page 103)

Digital

This refers to any system in which *data* is coded in the form of digits. (see *Binary*)

Digitiser

A device that converts non-digital *data* (e.g. text, images and sounds) into a *digital* format.

Directories

Hard disks and *floppy disks* can hold a great deal of *data*, stored as separate *files*. These *files* can be organised into different directories, which makes it easier to find them at a later date. (see page 107)

Electronic Mail (E-Mail)

This is used for the sending of messages between people who have *computers* which are linked together. The connection between *computers* can be direct via a *network*, or indirect via a *modem*. (see *Telecommunications*)

File

A file is a *program* or a collection of *data* that is stored on a disk.

Filename

When you save a *file* you must allocate a filename. Disk Operating Systems identify *files* and their locations using these filenames. (see page 107)

Floppy Disk

A disk, protected by a plastic casing, which is used to store *programs* and *data*. The advantage of *floppy disks* over *hard disks* is that they can be removed after use and they can be read from and written to many times. The disadvantage is that they do not hold much *data* (360K-2MB). The most common *floppy disks* are referred to as 5¼and 3½which is the actual diameter of the disk inside the casing.

Font

The style and size of a typeface. (see page 103)

Footers/Headers

Information that is entered at the bottom (foot) or top (head) of a document page.

Gigabyte (GB)

Originally the term for 1,024 *megabytes* (MB) or 1,048,576 *kilobytes* (K), but increasingly being used to mean 1000 *megabytes* or 1,000,000 *kilobytes*. (see *byte*)

Graphical User Interface (GUI)

These were developed in the mid-1980s to make *computers* easier to use for those with no technical training or experience. A GUI replaces the traditional method of typing in commands, with a pointing device. The pointing device (such as a *mouse*) is used to point and select icons that initiate *applications* or perform functions. GUIs are not an *operating system* in their own right, but an add-on to the resident *operating system*. Each manufacturer of GUIs uses conventions across all their *software* which allow you to become familiar with a variety of *applications* quickly, as they are all presented in the same manner. The creators of GUIs were Apple, although the best known GUI is Microsoft's Windows (see page 116).

Hard Disk

A Hard Disk (also known as a Hard Drive) is a combination of a disk for storing *data*, and a drive mechanism for reading and writing *data*. It is usually permanently fixed within a computer, although portable versions do exist. Hard disks have a much larger capacity (100MB-2GB) than a *floppy disk*. The access time and transfer rate is also far quicker than from a *floppy disk*.

Hardware

The physical equipment that forms a computer. Hardware consists of all the common computer components such as the keyboard, monitor and disk drive, and any additional pieces of equipment.

Hypertext

A method in which text that is highlighted within a document or application can be selected using a pointing device, and further information called up.

Import

A process by which *data* that has been created using one application is brought into another application. During the process, the *data* is usually translated into a format that the importing application can understand. Documents can be stored in a format that can be read by many *applications*. The most common of these formats is *ASCII*. The information that can be stored in these formats, however, is restricted. For example, *ASCII* allows the storage of characters, but *data* such as *fonts*, document styles and *footers/headers* may be lost in translation.

Indent

Setting text or an image in a document in from either the left or right-hand margin. (see page 119)

Information

Data that has been understood by a human being. (see *Data and Information*)

Information Technology

The use of micro-processor based equipment to process and communicate information. The emergence and coalition of micro-electronics, *computers* and *telecommunications* has resulted in the dramatic and widespread use of information technology. Information that uses information technology is always recorded and transmitted in the form of *digital data*. Therefore, typewriters or conventional radios, which handle information and employ technology are not examples of information technology as they do not use *digital data.*

Input

The entering of *data* into a computer.

Integrated Package

This refers to a suite of *applications*, usually consisting of a *word processor*, a *spreadsheet*, a *database*, and presentation *software*. There are three advantages to integrated packages. The first is that the *applications* look similar and, therefore, once one application is learnt, it is easier to learn the others. The second advantage is that integration allows you to combine the *applications* easily. For example, a document created in the *word processor* could be combined with a list of names and addresses from the *database.* The third advantage is that it is a cheap way of equipping your computer with *applications* because purchasing an integrated package is often not much more expensive than purchasing a single application.

Internet

A global federation of networked computers. The internet allows you to communicate with others through your computer and gives you access to a vast amount of information from other individual and corporate users.

Kilobyte

Originally the term for 1,024 *bytes* (=1K) but increasingly being used to mean 1000 *bytes*. (see *Byte*)

Macros

Routines that allow you to reduce long *procedures* to a single keystroke or *mouse* click. These can also be automated. (see *Automated Routines* and page 115)

Mail Merge

The action of combining a document with information from another *file.* The most common use of this is to combine a letter with a *database* of names and addresses.

Mainframe, Mini and Microcomputer Systems

The distinction between these *computer systems* is usually based upon the computing power (available memory and processing capability), the sophistication of the *operating system*, the number of *peripherals* and the number of users. Mainframes work very quickly, can perform many different tasks at once, and can support hundreds of terminals. Mainframe computers require special environments and skilled operators. A minicomputer has less power than a mainframe but is still very fast and capable of performing several tasks at once. A microcomputer is usually an isolated unit dependent upon a sole *microprocessor* chip. It is normally used by one person, running only one *program* at a time, although some powerful mirocomputers can run several *programs* at the same time.

Megabyte

Originally the term for 1,024 *kilobytes* (=1MB), but increasingly being used to mean 1000 *kilobytes* or 1,000,000 *bytes*. (see *byte*)

MHz (Megahertz)

Processor speed is described in terms of the number of electrical pulses that pass through a system in a second. *Microprocessors* achieve levels of several million pulses per second, and these are counted in megahertz (1,000,000 pulses = 1MHZ)

Microprocessor

The microprocessor, or *Central Processor Unit* (CPU), can be regarded as the engine of a *microcomputer*, which is often categorised by the type of processor it is using. Microprocessors are usually distinguished by the number of *bits* they can handle at a time: in general, the more *bits* they can handle, the faster they operate. The original IBM PC used an eight-bit processor, the Intel 8088. This has been followed by the 16-bit 80286 and the 32-bit 80386 and 80486 processors. The latest processor in this group is the

64-bit Pentium, which is capable of processing at speeds greater than 100 MHz. However, Intel have released details of a new chip codenamed the P6, and the technology surrounding processors is advancing rapidly.

MIDI

An acronym for Musical Instrument Digital Interface. This allows electronic musical instruments to communicate with the *computer* and with each other.

Modem

This allows two *computers* to communicate over the telephone network.

The mouse is the most common form of Pointing device...

Mouse

The most common form of pointing device. It is usually rectangular, and has one or more buttons. Moving the mouse across a surface results in the pointer on a *computers* monitor moving in a similar direction, and clicking the buttons allow icons or menu options to be selected.

Multimedia

Multimedia is the combination of two or more media. Multimedia on *computers* is the mixing of visual images, audio, and text. The most common medium for storing multimedia is the *CD-ROM* due to its large capacity (650MB) and cheap production cost.

Multi-tasking

The ability to have more than one *program* operating at the same time. In true multi-tasking, all *programs* can function at the same instant.

Network

A system of interconnections between *computers* that allow them to share *data* and resources, such as printers and *hard disks*. A network allows different users to pass *data* between them, but, if a network has many users, the exchange of *data* can become unacceptably slow.

Operating System

The *program* that handles *data* coming from and going to the many parts of a *computer*, such as the keyboard and *hard disk*. It also controls the actions of *programs* running on the *computer*. The most common operating system is DOS (Disk Operating System) and the most widely used DOS is Microsoft DOS (MS-DOS).

Output

Any *data* coming from a *computer* (e.g. information printed out, saved on disk, displayed on screen, or sent to another *computer*).

Password

A word or words known only to particular people which permit access to a *file* or *network*. They are used to restrict access for security reasons.

Peripherals

Additional pieces of *hardware* connected to, and controlled by, the *computer*. Strictly speaking the *hard disk* is a peripheral, but the term is now more commonly used for items outside the *computer* case, such as monitors and printers.

Procedures

In a *computer program*, a procedure is a routine that performs a particular function. Procedures can vary in complexity from simple addition of two numbers to more difficult calculations.

In the information-technology environment procedures are a set of actions which have been defined by an organisation or an individual and which must be adhered to. Examples include rules for naming of data *files* and methods for dealing with system faults.

Program

A sequence of codes that instruct a *computer's microprocessor* to perform certain tasks. A *computer* cannot perform any useful function without a program.

RAM

An acronym for Random Access Memory. This is the area of a *computer* that is used for storing temporary *data*, such as documents or *applications* which are being used. The contents of this memory can be altered, but are lost when the *computer* is turned off. For this reason RAM is said to be 'volatile'. If you wish to store something permanently you must save it onto a disk drive.

ROM

An acronym for Read Only Memory (i.e. you can read from it, but you cannot write to it or change it in any way). This is an area of memory which holds *programs* and *data* relevant to the running of the basic *computer*. ROM holds a permanent copy of these *programs* and *data* which are not erased when the *computer* is turned off.

Scanner

A device that converts images, such as photographs or drawings, into *binary* data. This *data* can then be read by specific *applications* to reproduce the image on the *computer* screen or print it out.

Software

Programs and *data* that are stored on disk.

Spreadsheet

An application for analysing numerical *data*. Spreadsheets can be used for many tasks from adding up a list of numbers to complex statistical forecasts. (see page 112)

RAM is said to be volatile....

Style Sheet

A term for a *template* in *word processing* or *desktop publishing* packages. (see *Template*)

Template

A saved framework that can be retrieved and used repeatedly. For example, you could set up a *spreadsheet* with a certain structure (template) which can be retrieved many times and filled in with different sets of *data*. In *word processing* and *desktop publishing*, templates (sometimes known as *style sheets* or master pages) can be defined for particular types of document - for example, fax cover sheets or memoranda.

Telecommunications

The transmission of *digital data* over distances by use of cables or via radio waves. Modern communications allow computers to transmit and receive *data* quickly, and without errors (including sound and moving images), by using complex techniques that compress the *data* and check that the *data* that arrives is the same as the *data* that was sent. The more widespread use of optical fibre cables and satellites, the use of ISDN (Integrated System Digital Network) and improvements in *Modems* have resulted in an increase in the speed at which this *data* is sent.

A number of services use telecommunications to allow you to connect with other computers for the purpose of sending and receiving mail, and accessing information. The *internet* is one example of a service.

Virtual Reality

This uses a *computer* to create a 3D 'world' which a person can explore using sophisticated video and sound equipment. This exploration involves wearing a headset, with miniature monitors for eyepieces, through which the artificial world is seen.

Virus

A *computer virus* is a *program* that can enter your *computer*, usually through a contaminated disk, and cause damage. (see page 109)

Windows

See *Graphical User Interface* and page 116.

Word Processor

See page 118

Write-Protect Tab

A notch in a *floppy disk* that can be moved in order to write-protect a disk so that the information contained on it cannot be changed. (see page 109)

WYSIWYG

An acronym for What You See Is What You Get which refers to an *applications* ability to accurately represent on screen what will be printed out. (see page 119)

Published in 1996 by Collins Education
An imprint of HarperCollins*Publishers*
77–85 Fulham Palace Road
Hammersmith
London
W6 8JB
© 1996 HarperCollins*Publishers*

Peter Robinson asserts the moral right to be identified as the author of this work.

Design and typesetting by Derek Lee
Cover Design by Derek Lee
Illustrated by Harry Venning
Printed and bound by Scotprint Ltd., Musselburgh
Commissioning Editor Graham Bradbury
Project Editor Lesley Young

Acknowledgements
The publishers would like to thank Boots the Chemist for all their help in the research for this book.

Note from the author
The author would like to thank his wife and children for their love and support. He would also like to thank Colin and Adele Friedland, proprietors of the Village Pharmacy, Hemel Hempstead who supplied advice and ideas; Jill Male and Carl Gregory from Mackworth College, Derby, for their insights into the Business curriculum; Jef Robinson who suggested and supplied much of the source data for the activities; the National Extension College who let him use the Oasis product line which originally appeared in their IT in Context resource pack; John Reeves and Jef Robinson for providing many valuable suggestions for improving the text; and the original editors Graham Bradbury, Allison Walters and Louisa Coulthurst, along with Lesley Young, for their commitment and, above all, their patience.